Taxi for Spirit 2

PURE GOLD

JEFFREY 'SHANTI' WOODCOCK

2QT Publishing

First Edition published 2022 by

2QT Publishing
Settle, North Yorkshire BD24 9RH United Kingdom

Copyright © Jeffrey "Shanti" Woodcock

The right of Jeffrey "Shanti" Woodcock to be identified as the author of this work has been asserted by him in accordance with the Copyright, Designs and Patents Act 1988

All rights reserved. This book is sold subject to the condition that no part of this book is to be reproduced, in any shape or form. Or by way of trade, stored in a retrieval system or transmitted in any form or by any means, electronic, mechanical, photocopying, recording, be lent, re-sold, hired out or otherwise circulated in any form of binding or cover other than that in which it is published and without a similar condition, including this condition being imposed on the subsequent purchaser, without prior permission of the copyright holder.

Printed by IngramSparks

Cover images: shutterstock.com
Taxi 'driver': Jeffrey Woodcock

A CIP catalogue record for this book is available from the British Library

ISBN - 978-1-914083-61-7

DEDICATION

I dedicate this book to my beautiful mum Louie and dad Roy for the many varied and challenging experiences that our souls have shared in this and other lifetimes. I love you so much. Thank you for these most sacred of moments.

I also dedicate this book to the many beautiful angels who have helped me on my journey, but none more so than Deborah and Yvonne.

When meeting Deborah in 2008 and Yvonne in 2005 these meetings were timed to perfection.

In 2008 I met Deborah just hours after I had spent an emotional time in hospital with Dad, who had just had a stroke.

In 2005 I met Yvonne a month after Mum had passed.

These two meetings were signs from heaven that help was here, for in each situation I was at rock-bottom, and I do mean rock-bottom.

Dad's stroke and his loss of speech set in motion a really challenging few years as his health deteriorated.

And Mum's death left me feeling so heartbroken, lost and alone that I honestly didn't think I would get through.

These two earth angels have helped me greatly in their own magical ways and I am so, so grateful and blessed to call these ladies the dearest of friends.

Deborah and Yvonne; I wish and pray that all your heart's desires come true. Thank you both for being in my life.

And while wishing this for these two angels, I also wish the same for you too.

Contents

Dedication	3
Foreword	9
Disclaimer	10
Archangel Michael's Divine Wisdom	11
Soul Retrieval: What Is It?	15

Part 1
Concluding Information from the SRs Written About in *Taxi for 'Spirit' - Diary of a Soul Retriever*

The Triceratops SR ~ Completed 22nd February 2021	24
The Meg SR ~ Completed 12th March 2021	26
The Braemar SR Completion ~ 1st June 2021 to 23rd June 2021	31
The Pictish Fort SR ~ 12th July to 14th July 2021	41
The *Titanic* SR ~ 19th & 20th December 2021	45

Part 2 - The New SRs

The Tower Block SR ~ 14th December 2020	49
The Impregnable Fortress SR ~ 12th to 15th March 2021	51
The Happy SR ~ from 2011 to 3rd May 2021	56
The Dementia SR ~ 13th May 2021 to 19th May 2021	58
A Mother and Father Dementia SR ~ 20th & 21st May 2021	65
Dementia: Additional Information ~ 18th & 19th June 2021	69
Trinity's Baptism into SR ~ May 2021 to 24th June 2021	76
The Ostracised SR ~ 24th & 25th June 2021	79

The Reptilian Race SRs ~ 16th June 2021 to 9th August 2021	85
My Brother Jack's SR ~ from 1964 to 31st July 2021	98
The Gas Chamber SR ~ from *circa* 1979 to 19th August 2021	102
The Crystal Magic SR ~ 15th August 2021	106
The Pain Release SR ~ from 2011 to 9th September 2021	107
The Multi-pickup SR ~ 13th September 2021	115
The Suicide Cycle SR ~ Date Unknown to 15th September 2021	119
Soul Retrieval Work ~ Moving to a New Level	124
The Cellar SR ~ 13th October 2021	128
Ouija Boards	135
The Aleister Crowley SR ~ 3rd August 2016 to 15th October 2021	137
The Dr Zhivago SR ~ 17th October 2021	143
The Swift SR ~ 21st October 2021	148
Everything Is Energy	151
The Revenge SR ~ 1400s to 2nd November 2021	156
The Abandonment SR ~ Date Unknown to 3rd November 2021	163
The Night of a Thousand SRs ~ 15th & 16th November 2021	168
The Massage Bed SR ~ 22nd & 23rd November 2021	173
The Anonymous SR ~ from BCE to 18th January 2022	176
The Footballer's SR ~ from 26th to 29th November 2021	181
The Soulmate SR ~ from BCE to 8th December 2021	184
The Ardlui & Loch Lomond SR ~ from July 2017 to 17th December 2021	190
The Pure Gold SR ~ from Around 2000 BCE to 22nd February 2022	197

The Remember 'The Promise You Made' SR ~ September 1999 to 10th February 2022	202
The Ancestral & Reptilian SR ~ Date Unknown to 10th March 2022	212
A Message from Jesus	216
A General Recap	223
A Soul Retriever's Toolkit (Guidelines, Updated)	230
Important, additional information	233

Foreword

BOOK ONE WAS my 'early school years' book. But writing this second book, while it expands on the way I am doing SR work now, has made me realise that I am still learning and remembering. I am also adding more of the detailed information that I feel will benefit you as you expand your own SR journey or just your curiosity in general. And I'm tying up many, if not all, loose ends in the process.

As we realise through our spiritual awakening who we truly are, we see the delights that are on offer. The rewards are truly great in many expansive, expected, and unexpected ways. The more I share my life experiences with you the more I hope you will be able to see the beauty within you, whatever you have experienced in life.

At times it has been very challenging indeed, and while I would, on a human level, change many things, on a soul level everything has happened perfectly.

It's all good, and it is all part of your soul's ongoing journey of rediscovery of who you truly are.

Disclaimer

REGARDING ANY PASSAGE in this book where I share information regarding any specific health, emotional or mental issue, ailment or illness... These are my personal spiritual views and beliefs and mine alone, from my many and varied experiences.

I urge you to trust your instincts. Do whatever resonates in a positive way within you.

If it doesn't resonate with you let it go. Do what you feel is the best for you, for your body and for your spiritual journey. I can only share my experiences with you, and how I have come to understand my own body and what it can cope with.

This is what I do urge you to do: make the decisions that best suit you and your body to bring you peace of mind. You know your body better than anyone else.

This in part, is the way to taking our power back.

Archangel Michael's Divine Wisdom

I PLACE THIS information at the top of the list because I feel the sooner you read it the sooner it will assist you in all areas of your life. Use this method to help people, but also keeping on the right side of the spiritual boundaries, because if we step over them we create more karma for ourselves, even though our only desire is to help.

It is only natural to want to help our family and close friends, or indeed anyone we meet or know who might be going through the sort of unnecessary situations that we have been through. It's only natural to want to save those people from going through what we have experienced.

This was one of the hardest realisations that I came to understand and accept during Dad's illness. I tried all the spiritual ways I knew to prevent him experiencing an unpleasant situation, but by doing this I was interfering in his soul's journey. My actions, although pure in intention, were affecting Dad's soul journey. So I, through my intentions, created karma for myself in the process.

In the end Dad still ended up going through the

unpleasant situation which, as I now accept, had to happen for Dad, me, and the person we were to meet. It was part of our soul contract, which ended when meeting a doctor at a Manchester hospital. It was as simple as that. But through my actions in trying to save Dad from a specific issue, we would have had to come back into another lifetime to clear that issue, had I succeeded. Thankfully my angelic friends got through to me and convinced me to let go and to allow Dad and his soul to experience his chosen path, which has benefited my soul too.

So how do we get around this situation to be able to help our loved ones without overstepping the spiritual boundaries? Well...

During a healing with my dear friend Yvonne, Archangel Michael came through Yvonne and shared her experience, which held some vital information. I have come to understand why my past experiences, which are helping me greatly at this time, may not be wholly relevant to you. But you will undoubtedly benefit from heeding what comes next if you choose to. And as you open spiritually you will come to realise that your past-life experiences are blessings here to help you in the present.

I spoke to Yvonne about a SR I have written about further on in this book, the cellar SR, and that I had in some way taken on some of the emotion and pain experienced by one or more of the souls involved. Yvonne explained that she had already been through this learning process and that we don't need to take on anything unnecessary from those who we are helping through our spiritual work, be it emotional, mental or physical.

Yvonne explained how Archangel Michael put the question to her in a way that allowed her to arrive at an amicable conclusion in her own way. He put it to Yvonne in a way that she would understand and, in time, act on. This all occurred with Archangel Michael staying well within the spiritual boundary.

The way he put it to Yvonne was something like this. 'Do you feel you benefit from taking on these unnecessary emotions?'

When Yvonne understood this question she realised all she needed to do was ask, be it Archangel Michael or any other angel for specific help in any way. This made her spiritual work a lot easier to complete without causing her physical body to go through unnecessary pain-releasing.

It's the same for me and you too, if we choose.

As Yvonne told me this I remembered and realised why I had gone to the Samaritans and offered my services just after Mum had passed. I was with the Samaritans for around a year. During this time I answered many phone calls from people in great despair. The main rule to remember when volunteering for the Samaritans is that you are there to listen and to listen only. However, there are ways to navigate around that. You can put certain thoughts to the caller by putting a question back to them in a certain way. This would still leave the power of choice in their hands but would provoke thoughts that they may not have had.

Here are some examples:
  Have you ever thought about trying?
  What do you think about this?
  Do you think this may help?

I'm sure you can think of other ways in which to express yourself in the same manner.

It's all about putting a question to a person in a way that gives them the opportunity to decide for themselves about something that they would not necessarily have thought of, especially when going through trauma, or emotional or mental challenges, without taking their power away and without stepping over the spiritual boundary.

This is so important as we set sail on our spiritual journey.

Soul Retrieval: What Is It?

SOUL RETRIEVAL IS simply the reconnecting of one part of a soul to its other part(s) to eventually make it whole. I will use my soul, Shanti, as an example (Shanti is the spiritual name of my soul).

My soul is, and has been, on an everlasting journey of rediscovery of who and what it truly is: a pure being of love and light. My soul has visited this planet many times and has had many experiences as it has progressed, lifetime after lifetime.

During my soul's journey it has experienced the darkest of times and the happiest of times, which have all caused my soul to experience every emotion possible on earth.

On some occasions the experiences have been too challenging for my soul and it has experienced great discomfort and great happiness, leading up to the passing of my physical body.

Whether it be through love, fear, sadness or happiness, our soul can find it too hard to let go completely. So part of the soul can become trapped in the moment.

In truth, it all boils down to one feeling: fear. Even when passing in a happy state, a trapped soul may well choose to stay because it fears that there is nothing better than the happiness it has just experienced.

Over a period of visits to this planet my soul has split into more than one piece.

I know this to be true, for the healings I have experienced with Yvonne have shone light upon many of these lifetimes, where she has ventured back to the place where a specific part of my soul has been trapped. Through many healings Yvonne has been instrumental in these lifetimes, and the information she has shared with me from them is now proving to be invaluable.

With Yvonne's tutorage, I have attained the level of being able to learn of and visit these past lifetimes myself, so it's a win–win situation. Thank you, Yvonne.

Here is one priceless example Yvonne shared with me.

During a healing, Yvonne was taken to Rosslyn Castle (not to be confused with Rosslyn Chapel) where she found my soul standing to attention near a ruined wall. Yvonne knew that the castle in its true state was in ruins. However, my soul was trapped in an illusion. My soul believed that it was still protecting a fully functioning castle. Yvonne said to me after the healing, 'It took a while to convince your soul of this, but I did eventually.'

The outcome was that the part of my soul once trapped at Rosslyn Castle will have, through Yvonne's help, moved on, and will have returned to heaven or to a beautiful realm to recuperate before being safely reunited with the largest part of my soul at some point in the future.

It's just like piecing together a jigsaw puzzle, and no harm befalls your current physical body as you awaken to this phenomenon. A soul retrieval can be experienced while you sleep, and you will know nothing of it when you awake. On waking you may well begin to remember where your soul has been and what it has experienced. It can also occur during a one-to-one healing session through any number of natural healing therapies, such as reiki (any of the many different versions of this healing technique) shamanic healing or any number of other natural healing modalities as I experienced with Yvonne.

However, for me – and more excitingly – it can be done at the actual site of a historic or a prehistoric event or at someone's home or workplace.

This is why this book has been created: to share with you my many varied, wonderful, magical and fantastic soul retrieval experiences. Within this amazing team of angels I am the conduit for heaven and earth to bring both together to help one or many souls return in one fell swoop.

When called to be of service in this way, I am in my element. I simply love helping souls in this way, and if my physical body were willing I would do this twenty-four hours a day, every day, for the rest of my tenure here on earth. I would be a very happy bunny indeed.

Alas, our physical body does need a little time to recover from the exertions of this wonderful work. To help you become more open-minded about this type of spiritual experience, it might be an idea to see if you can relate to anything involving déjà vu. This can be a fleeting moment in which you recognise a place, a person or a clip from a scene in your life that is yet to be played out. Or it could be a place or person you are very familiar with but know you haven't met in this present lifetime.

All these experiences point to previous encounters here on earth. I have had a few of these moments throughout my life, but over the last few months they have happened more frequently. Again, they are nothing to be fearful of. In fact, I find them very comforting, for I see them as signs that I'm on the right track on my life's journey.

There are a few outcomes to these retrieval experiences that have all been perfect. For my part, I know that whatever I am meant to do I do complete my mission during any soul retrieval. I know that this is the case via many signs that appear to confirm this.

There may well be souls who choose to stay, simply because another soul retriever has agreed to reconnect with them at the appropriate time. There is also a scenario whereby the soul can become trapped while the physical body is still alive and healthy. This occurs when a physical body experiences great trauma, shock, fear or loss in any life experience.

This I refer to as an essence.

Essence: this is simply the residue of a person's memory which, over time, will create a build-up of specific emotions and feelings in a specific place. The longer a person has stayed in one specific place (for example, where they have lived) these essences become stronger, especially if their experience is powerful enough emotionally, mentally, or physically. Most of the time it will be a combination of all three.

Any situation that creates enough fear, drama or trauma for the physical body can cause part of our soul to stay put. The soul will opt for safety. Again, as with all other forms of soul retrieval, I will add my experiences of this type of situation in this book too.

Another way soul retrieval can be necessary occurs when we form an attachment to close friends or family. We love them so deeply that when they pass we can subconsciously hold on to a part of their soul, and this holds them here on earth.

We don't consciously know this until a time when we are spiritually aware of this type of experience, or when the trapped soul is ready to move on. However, when this happens it is for us to let go, for this part of our loved one's soul is ready to move on, especially when they start making noises, which get our attention very clearly and loudly in some cases.

When I do a soul retrieval of this nature, I specifically explain to the person who has asked for my help that while it is necessary I assure them they will still have a connection to their loved one(s), but a healthier one.

This is their reward for allowing the soul that has attached itself to them to move on and to return to the light or to heaven to be healed. When any form of soul retrieval is complete, this part of the soul can then reconnect to the main part of their soul – sometimes with immediate effect – wherever it may be and whatever it may be experiencing, without the baggage of the emotions and feelings attached to the lifetime they were trapped in. Sometimes the soul will be taken to a healing temple to receive healing before coming back into the fray.

This is what soul retrieval is all about.

In my case it's all about Shanti, the soul part of our union. He is on a journey. I play my part too (as the vehicle for the soul), and like any good team we both have our gifts, which complement one another.

Here are a few pointers and definitions that will make reading this book easier for you:

Soul(s): this is my chosen term for those trapped. There are other words you could use if you wish, such as *spirit*, or even *ghost*, but I must stick with one word and follow it through, so that you are not confused.

When I say *soul*(s) I do mean only a part of their soul(s), because the soul itself can be dissected into many parts and become trapped in many different lifetimes along its journey.

This is an important piece of information to take in when reading further into this book. I know this may be a tad confusing, but the title for the book sounds better with the word *spirit* rather than *soul*. The title is the only time I have used the word *spirit*.

SR: this is short for *soul retrieval*.

EC: this is short for *essence clearing*.

Move-on: this is the term I have chosen to use for the trapped soul(s) leaving this planet. Other terms, such as going home, *going back to the light or going back to heaven* may be more comforting for you to use in place of move on.

Brucie Bonus: a phrase I use which I heard frequently

on a TV programme, it simply means an added bonus/blessing to the already magical gifts I received throughout my spiritual journey.

As the SR experiences multiply, so does my wealth of knowledge, which you will obviously see through the explanation of each SR as my experience and my confidence grow.

Helping trapped souls move on and find peace is an honour. I am so blessed. This is my soul's purpose. So without further ado, please read on.

Part 1

Concluding Information from the SRs
Written About in Book One

The Triceratops SR ~ Completed 22nd February 2021

THIS DAY BROUGHT down the curtain on an amazing issue that has spanned quite a long time.

Over the previous weekend I had visited Gina, and a short while later we were joined by Eve (both these names are aliases).

Eventually, during our chat, the lifetime my soul experienced as a baby triceratops came to the fore. I knew Gina's soul was the *T. rex* that had initially taken a chunk out of my bum. But, to my astonishment, in a good way, I was to learn that Eve's soul resided within another *T. rex*, which finished me off. The baby triceratops died from this second attack.

Again, how things come together at the perfect time is always surprising. Since the moment I met Eve, who is part of a reiki share and angel group that has been going for a good while now, I was aware that we didn't really get on, even when Eve came to Gina's and sat on the settee next to me. I had no idea what I had done, but subconsciously I must have felt uncomfortable, and I tried to sit as far away from Eve on the settee as possible.

Obviously there was something underlying that needed attending to, but having been brought together, as we had been, we were able to forgive each other, for my soul may well have caused Eve's soul some discomfort through other lifetimes too. So this was truly karma being balanced.

It only took sixty million years, give or take a year, but at least the karma is balanced now.

The Meg SR ~ Completed 12th March 2021

THIS ADDITIONAL INFORMATION came via a lady who contacted me to do a distant SR for her. The first time I spoke on the phone with her I sensed that she was very wary and unsure about getting in touch with me, so there was no follow-up. Thankfully she did get in touch a few weeks later. This will be explained shortly.

I have left the lady nameless, for she has no need to be made aware of this issue. It would only bring unnecessary emotion up for her.

During the chat I began to receive a picture of what was to be done but had no inclination that it was connected to Meg (the town of Metheringham) as we chatted.

I instigated the SR to begin as I settled down for sleep, feeling it needed Shanti my soul to play a part.

I woke up at 5.55 a.m. and realised that I was being gifted some information regarding the issue at hand, which did indeed involve Shanti, and which all stemmed from his lifetime's experience in Meg.

As the information flowed in I began to understand

why this lady had been very cautious in contacting me, for her soul had played a pivotal role in Meg. There had been a terrible fire there. Her soul resided within the person who had accidentally started the fire, but through fear or for whatever reason she had pointed the finger at me. This is what the lady had felt when first phoning me. No wonder she needed time to gather herself before the second attempt at contact.

The lady's soul in the life in Meg was a young girl who was a childhood friend of my soul's incarnation, a little boy. She and her family had held a powerful position in this small community, so when the finger was pointed at the little boy for starting the fire, nothing he said or did would appease the angry crowd. They chose to believe the young girl instead. Now I understand why the little boy cursed as he was unpleasantly put to death.

All this was connected to a feeling of, 'What have I done wrong?'

The lady had obviously reached a level of awareness where she had started to listen to her soul's guidance, even though she had no idea what she was getting in touch for. I'm so glad she did.

Finally, we could bring an amicable end to this lifetime. It was time for her to own up and to seek forgiveness, for the guilt would have been weighing heavily on her shoulders in this present lifetime. It was for Shanti and me to also forgive, which we did. The lady, without knowing why, will now feel lighter, after having let go of many lifetimes' worth of guilt. This was her blessing.

Finally knowing now what led to my death in that lifetime is a great relief and is another one we can put on the closed pile. This was my blessing.

Additional information gained on 29th November 2021.

On the powerful 11/11 gateway during an informal chat with friends a subject came up about a lifetime that Yvonne's soul experienced, a very unpleasant one with an unpleasant ending.

As I listened I became more and more uncomfortable because I knew it involved my soul, and I knew what my soul's actions had caused. Yvonne and I have spoken of this lifetime on the odd occasion, which has brought about complete forgiveness on both sides.

While my soul in this instance was the instigator of Yvonne's soul's experiences, the roles have also been reversed. Yvonne's soul and my soul have experienced being both the instigator and victim. Hence the reason why the forgiveness was so easily forthcoming.

The point of this latest addition is that my soul got away with his actions. When I say that he got away with his actions it means that he didn't get caught by the authorities. However, as with any unloving action, thought or word spoken we create karma. My soul certainly created much karma for his actions in this lifetime's experience.

The underlying issue for my soul's many reincarnations in various physical bodies after this lifetime was this: it would have felt exactly how those who were resident in Metheringham felt during the fire, but they would have had no idea where those feelings were coming from. My soul's physical bodies, Jeffrey's included, had been subconsciously waiting for someone to come back from the past to seek revenge for what had happened.

Just as with those souls in Metheringham, they were in anticipatory fear until I and Shanti went back – not to seek revenge but to heal the whole issue, so all the souls could move on from that lifetime.

This is what I have been feeling for many years since this lifetime with Yvonne first came to light. I have been in a state of anticipatory fear. Thankfully this is no longer true, as Yvonne had changed the way she reacted. More importantly, she didn't react.

This is how we break the cycles. Thankfully Yvonne instigated this cycle's ending through her forgiveness, rather than continuing to create karma for herself and hurting our loved ones – who were involved on the periphery of this cycle, which our souls had created.

It is the 1st December 2021 as I sit typing. Yesterday evening I, after receiving many signs, realised that this lifetime would require a SR to complete it. My soul had become trapped, due to the ever-growing fear of being caught, which had led to my physical body in this particular lifetime committing suicide. I have mentioned this cycle before, and this lifetime was ensconced within it. Thus, my soul created the same ending as in previous lives and indeed after this lifetime, until I was blessed with the spiritual awareness to bring it to a close – which, thankfully, I did during this SR.

And the SR happened at the perfect time. As with all things, a sequence is to be followed and adhered to, so the 11/11 gateway (a specific day a portal for divine energies to infuse the earth opens, there are a few throughout the year, like 1/1 the 1st of January and so on) was the event that set in motion a chain reaction, a gentle yet challenging passage of spiritual work that led to yesterday evening's SR. The blessings I have been showered with are many, but none is more important than the experiencing of the emotional turmoil and the mental strain that this experience has shown me.

I have a greater understanding now regarding those souls in Metheringham and how they were affected from the moment they were cursed and how those feelings of fear escalated over generations for them. Since the 11/11 gateway I have subtly been feeling these emotions and feelings grow, causing more and more fear, panic and such feelings of vulnerability that have been quite scary even for me, to the point where I have been wary of venturing out of my home over the last week or so.

But that was only until the very strong appearance energetically of my soul from that life.

The Braemar SR Completion ~ 1st June 2021 to 23rd June 2021

THIS ADDITIONAL SR has surprised me as much as it may surprise you.

From the beginning of June 2021, changes have occurred in my personal life that have led me to distance myself from a person with whom I was in a toing and froing situation. I was also feeding their craving. So I took the option to step back, to no longer invite the negativity to ooze out from this person – for their benefit even more than for mine.

If we keep giving energy to a negative situation or event, through a spoken word or a thought, then we are keeping ourselves attached to the situation, which renders us unable to move forward. So my decision to step back has been a positive move for both of us.

Whether the person involved has found someone else to dance with or not ... that is their choice.

I, on the other hand, have chosen to no longer be involved. But during the last few weeks I have felt something stirring, something I was unable to put my finger on until yesterday evening, the 17th June.

I knew it was something unpleasant because the one time I tried to do some SR work I was left with a feeling that nothing had been achieved, which was a strange feeling. However, I must remember this statement...

> Everything is in divine and perfect order, always.

And so again this statement was to prove correct. I had a healing at Yvonne's on 16th June, which happened to be my birthday. But, even then, extraordinarily little information came to me. Again, this was a very strange occurrence, especially because I was with Yvonne, because our coming together during healing sessions always seems to bring up everything for healing – even stuff I'd never thought about. Anyway, it was all another part of my learning regarding SR that I must accept and do gladly.

Also during the last few weeks, I have found it extremely hard to trust the person mentioned above. In fact it has become harder the longer this issue has stayed hidden. It has nothing to do with the person who is involved with this SR. It is their soul, so the person has had no idea what was unfolding over this period. This is a good thing, really.

So returning to yesterday evening, the 17th June 2021... I was watching an episode of *Death in Paradise*, a police crime series set in the Caribbean. This episode showed me what I needed to see.

In Braemar I had, as it turns out, a younger sister called Patricia. After our parents were murdered for their wealth both Patricia and I were placed in the care of those who had murdered them. After the programme I sensed a soul make their presence felt. It was my sister. Her death in the Braemar lifetime was also a very unpleasant one, which my soul had been forced to witness.

Having witnessed this I must have made a run for it. Hence the recurring dream of running through a forest unable to speak for the fear that surfaced after having witnessed this atrocious act. It was a ritual performed by a satanic cult, which as I have previously said also ended my life in Braemar.

A while later I found out that the soul of my sister in this lifetime was part of Debbie's soul. Debbie is a very close friend in this lifetime, and we have a close soul connection going back possibly to the beginning of time. It has been and still is an extraordinarily strong bond. In truth it is a soulmate connection (this is not to be confused with a soulmate cum twin flame connection).

To explain...

Debbie and I are from the same soul group, which is a group that reincarnates many times in many different experiences to help one another's souls evolve. A twin flame connection is the feminine and masculine part of the same soul coming together. This is happening currently to help with the raising of the vibration of the earth, for when a twin flame union occurs it enhances the other person's gifts, which make it a more powerful combination.

So for my soul as a child to have witnessed this abhorrent act against my sister, who was also a soulmate, obviously caused me great heartache and pain, which then caused me to become incredibly angry at those who had caused this dreadful untold suffering.

This is the reason why I have been unable to trust the person over the last few weeks. Their soul was the high priestess of the cult that caused all this suffering to my family.

Because of the deceit, the betrayal and the breach of trust that occurred in this past lifetime, I can well understand why I was unable to trust them in the here and now.

I state again that the person's physical body has no idea this has happened in a past life. And they will remain oblivious to this information, with God's gracious help.

Now I have all the pieces of the jigsaw, after having pieced them together in a way that I resonate and trust what has been written, I can now move into Phase 2 of this SR.

All the unpleasantness happened in the past, so it cannot be changed, but the cycle can be ended. I choose to forgive those involved to bring this cycle to an end. And, as strange as it may seem, it was all part of the journey our souls chose to experience. Even the most horrible experiences were part of it. So it is time to let go of the past and move on.

Today, 18th June, I have had one heck of a busy morning during intermittent spells of sleep. I have been to visit two crystal shops and had a lovely time with Jaime, Trinity and Beth, who run the two shops, which then set me up in readiness to do the final SR at Rivington, a place that is becoming a portal for many souls to move on. It really is a beautiful spot, so why not?

Since yesterday evening Patricia and I have been talking. After helping her see that she is in no more danger from that lifetime, I also felt that I had to ask her to forgive me for not being able to protect her from those experiences. I spoke to Patricia about forgiving those who did those things to her in that lifetime to help set herself free – which would in turn set their souls free too. Sometimes this can feel like those who have done the dirty deed are being let off scot-free, though.

But in truth we are all connected, and to set their souls free is the same as setting our souls free. But they will have incurred karma regardless, which is all part of their souls' earth experience.

Someone must set the ball rolling regarding ending any specific cycle, otherwise we would go round and round forever, which is not a pleasant thought.

Now I am sitting down at Rivington, with the information that my SR friends had already put in place a ring of divine light around the area and were awaiting our arrival. This had never happened before, and it left me quite amazed.

I began the SR but was soon taken away from the actual SR after being given further information to write about, as I am doing now. I was taken away from this simply because of the deep soul connection with Debbie's soul and with Patricia in Braemar. Because there is no such thing as loss I had no need to step back into that emotion.

Moments later I was gifted a sign that the SR had been completed, via a deep feeling of peace and calmness. A win–win situation had occurred. My soul connection with Debbie's soul has become stronger in a healthier way because of this SR having healed the unhealthy issues and left the door open for unconditional love to flow in. A much better soul connection has been achieved.

A few days later, on the 23rd June 2021

Once the SR for my sister Patricia was done and dusted, I really thought that was it. But boy, was I mistaken. On Sunday 20th June I arrived back home to find the owner of the house in my room, without an invitation.

This startled me somewhat. But thankfully, the previous few hours spent at a friend's had allowed the angels to get me into a calmer frame of mind, for they knew what was about to happen. My reaction to finding the owner in my room was very subdued. Again thankfully, I did express my disdain in a calm manner, but in such a way that I would incur no additional karma through my actions and words.

This experience was enough to trigger the deepest core emotions that remained connected to this lifetime. I would find out later today, 23rd June, the trapped soul from the distant SR I did a few years ago involved with Braemar had not, as I had thought, moved on. He was waiting for his sister – or, more specifically, the trapped part of her soul that I had connected with while at Debbie's a short while before. He was making sure that she was escorted to safety via a SR before making his final appearance.

The fact that my soul had waited all this time for the trapped part of Debbie and Patricia's soul to be found is quite understandable. For the soul of my dear friend Debbie and my soul Shanti have incarnated together many times, and in many of them my soul was an admirer and a protector of the physical body that Debbie's soul incarnated in. When I found out that my soul was waiting until Debbie's soul was safe and sound in the lifetime I am writing about, acting as her protector makes perfect sense to me. And in some ways it helps my soul to forgive himself for not being physically able to protect her in the Braemar lifetime.

This morning I meditated with my Arcturian friends, which was a catalyst for today's amazing experiences. I was finding it increasingly difficult to forgive the owner of the house for coming into my room uninvited. My mind was all a blur, creating all sorts of scenarios, and I wanted to face the owner and have it out.

I spoke very briefly to her as I left the house. Her parting shot was a look of great anger. I do not know if she saw me look at her, but it does not really matter.

It was a look that Dad used to give me before I left for various healing sessions with Yvonne. A part of Dad knew where I was going and what I was about to do, as did the owner of the house, which would bring about unwanted change within their reality. Each time I came back from a healing with Yvonne, Dad's demeanour was always one of deep peace, if only very briefly, so I know that the owner will feel the benefit, as Dad always did, after the events of today.

Both Dad and the owner's physical body may still act the same. But on a soul level I know, through messages that have come through Yvonne in the past and lately directly to me, that Dad, now in spirit, understands that everything I did was for his benefit too and that he was so grateful that I persevered, regardless of his state of mind. The same will be said for the owner's soul or higher self.

On both counts I will say nothing to the owner, just as I said nothing to Dad, because there is no point. Neither would have understood. Indeed, if I had, it may have created frightening thoughts within them. Again, there is no point in saying anything if it's going to cause upset.

On my arrival at Rivington and even during the early stages of my walk today I was oblivious to what was about to occur. I had felt cold the last few days but had put that down to the energies that were coming in from the summer solstice on 21st June.

As I neared the area that was now becoming more familiar to me as a portal for the SRs, past and future, I sensed that my SR teammates had already placed a small circle of light around the wooden bench I sit on during these magical experiences. Normally the circle of light would engulf the whole of the valley, but this time it was only big enough to surround me while in a sitting position.

I started to talk to the trapped part of my soul from this lifetime to tell him to let go of the anger, to forgive and to break the curse, to drop the thought of seeking revenge, to be the better man, and that no one was getting one over on him.

The curse was created silently as he was tortured to death. It's all about the intent. Whether the words are spoken or created within the mind they are still immensely powerful.

These are the feelings I had been experiencing over the last few days, and at an increasing rate too. This is because the longer the trapped soul stays with our physical body, the more likely we are to begin to take on the characteristics of the soul or the person's emotions, until we allow the releasing to flow from our physical body. However, if we do not release them, or we do not know how to release them, we can experience the emotions ourselves, and this is one reason why we become ill.

I have written a piece about hereditary in *Taxi for 'Spirit' - Diary of a Soul Retriever*, so please do check it out if you wish for a timely refresher.

When a lifetime is experienced such as this, those who have been wronged may seek revenge when there is no need to. Karma takes care of that. Not in an unpleasant way, for karma in my humble view is simply giving us another opportunity to alter the way we react to a similar situation the next time it comes around. Obviously if we create a massive amount of karma, with many souls, as my soul has done in the past, it can take a while to clear and balance the karma. Thankfully, through my physical body and my soul in the very recent past, we are working diligently to clear this backlog.

Any unkind actions, thoughts or words spoken create karma. So to kill or to sacrifice other human beings creates a larger portion of karma – which the souls involved in this lifetime will have accrued, make no mistake. So there really is no need to seek revenge, for we will only incur karma for ourselves if we do.

Today I realised that I connected with this part of my soul when leaving Braemar after my first visit. Receiving a phone call from Debbie just moments after leaving the hotel got me to stop the car, for what I thought was going to take my mind off the unpleasant experience in the hotel. But in fact it was to keep me in a static position long enough for the trapped soul to enter my car and to connect with me.

As I have said, this part of my soul was savagely killed in the woods. Where I stopped the car was obviously the place where my soul died. This is how precise our angelic guides can be in guiding us perfectly to any specific place on earth where we need to be for any number of specific reasons. The reason I had stopped there is perfectly understandable now, although I had to bear in mind that it had happened at least 300 years ago so the terrain would have looked quite different then.

For Braemar, on a personal level, the curtain has been brought down for the final time. But I still feel that there is SR work to be done there, especially in and around the castle, for I believe this is where this lifetime was mostly experienced and where most of the unholy acts took place.

Be assured, dear friends, that I will let you know how my visit goes, if and when I am guided to go. I do feel it will be an experience never to forget, just as the Boleskine SR was.

The Pictish Fort SR ~ 12th July to 14th July 2021

THE AMAZING CONCLUSION to this SR surfaced during a marathon healing session with Yvonne on 12th July 2021.

Many issues were brought up, and this was just one of them. After the healing Yvonne told me that in another life I had been impaled from the base to the crown of my head. But because this did not kill me quickly enough, the murderers proceeded to plunge a sword into my side, just for good measure.

Yvonne then asked me if I knew anyone who did this sort of horrific thing. Right away I said that there was a man named Vlad the Impaler, from whom the Dracula legend had allegedly originated, however this as the headline suggests involved a Pictish gentleman.

(Vlad the Impaler has since come up in another SR I have recently done April 2022 yet to be written about in book 3 possibly)

As Yvonne continued, she had to pull the sword out very slowly because it was taking my soul from that lifetime a little while to forgive the murderers. I wonder why.

When the forgiveness was offered by my soul, the sword was removed then replaced point down from my heart chakra downwards. Although this sword had been used to kill me in that life, I was then told that it is now the sword of truth, which will help me during my SR work in the future...

This was absolutely amazing, but the best is yet to come.

I now move to the morning of 14th July. The day before I had left the house where I was living for the last time and had headed to Whitby for a few days' rest and recuperation, or so I hoped. I had been out of sorts since leaving on the Monday morning through to this morning 14th of July, and I would soon understand why.

I kept getting an indistinct vision of me driving a few miles to Saltburn-by-the-Sea. So off I went. I had no real idea why until parking up. Seeing the beach without having to descend a few hundred metres, which sometimes you are obliged to at Whitby was a bonus. My angels were saving me some energy. I headed straight on to the beach, removing my shoes and socks in the process. I again asked my angels what was going on. What was causing my stressful situation?

I did not have too long to wait. Suddenly, I received the word *Pictish* in my mind's eye. I had no preconceived idea regarding this word, so took it as divine guidance. This set the ball rolling.

As I stood in the shallow water having a paddle I was taken back to the day before, when I had just arrived in

Whitby. It was over three years since I was last there, so I went to my usual haunts to see the people I knew from times past. Everything had changed. This seemed to heighten my stress levels (I have had problems in the past in accepting change of any type).

During this initial visit to the centre of Whitby, I walked down a narrow street and found a coffee shop, so I ordered some food and a coffee.

While I was eating a gentleman came in with a unique dress style. He was wearing a short dress or skirt and, while I did not focus fully, I believe he was completely dressed in women's clothing. I had no problem with that at all, but when I looked up I immediately felt sick. The reason for this would unravel on 14th July too.

So let's return to the beach and the paddling. Having received the word *Pictish*, I was soon shown the SR I did at Burghead in Scotland. This is where the deadly deed took place, right by the fort that I had done the SR on. Even though it had taken place well before the fort was built, it had happened on the same spot used by the Pictish ancestors during the Roman occupation of Britain.

Now, had I known about this additional information, would I have done the SR? I would, but it would have been very tough knowing what had happened to my soul in another lifetime. This reinforces the sentiment that everything is in divine and perfect order.

I did not have the experience or the understanding to do the SR when visiting Burghead. My angelic friends knew this, so only now – today – was I ready to complete this SR with the forgiveness necessary (which in truth had been given during the healing on Monday). However, the SR was to help me release the physical pain and emotional scars that I had unknowingly held since my visit to Burghead and the Pictish fort.

This is precisely why my angelic friends said nothing about the SR I did today while on the beach at Saltburn-by-the-Sea. And what an amazing SR it was.

As I began the SR inviting my SR friends to be present, I was also blessed with the appearance of two mermaids. They too were only too glad to help with this SR and, after all, as I found out later, the Roman (my soul from the other lifetime), when finally dying, was thrown into the sea, where I do believe the mermaids were waiting to take care of my soul and any others who leave a part of their soul behind until someone such as you or I return to finally complete the SR.

I believe this is part of their mission. What a wonderful SR to be part of.

The *Titanic* SR ~ 19th & 20th December 2021

THE LATEST INFORMATION came yesterday evening via a video sent to me by Debbie. It was a short video about how the *Titanic* really came to its tragic end. I have questioned the validity of the original reason for this tragedy for a long time. But enough about that. I'm not getting involved with the politics surrounding this event, so I will go back to the SR.

The video helped me gain more information regarding Dad and our lives in this lifetime – and that we were millionaires, thanks to Dad's business acumen. However, with the sinking of the *Titanic*, Dad was taken from us, as he went down with the ship. But all our wealth gained in that lifetime also went down into Davy Jones's locker.

This is the issue I need to attend to. The loss of our wealth from this lifetime and others ... for this, like other situations, has been a cycle spanning many lifetimes. I had a feeling of being cheated out of my inheritance and the feeling that one day I may even attempt to go down to the seabed and retrieve what is rightfully mine. I know that physically going to where the *Titanic* rests will never happen, but these are the underlying feelings that were attached to this lifetime and have affected me manifesting wealth and prosperity up to this point in this present lifetime.

Thankfully they are now a thing of the past.

Cord-cutting, EC and complete forgiveness have been the actions for me to take rather than doing a SR to bring this lifetime to a very timely end. I instigated these actions last night and again while at the seaside today. Boy, do I feel much lighter, after having let go of all the emotions and feelings ensconced within my soul's spiritual baggage.

A Brucie Bonus (originally from the Bruce Forsyth show *Play Your Cards Right*) for me is that I have now cleared a pathway for true abundance and prosperity to fully flow into my life now, without any fear of it being taken from me or any fear of losing it. No longer will I sabotage myself subconsciously through these now redundant thoughts and beliefs.

This most recent information via the video and my angelic friend's guidance has come at the perfect time as I prepare for the most amazing lifetime my soul has ever experienced, which goes all the way back to the triceratops life and even before that. It may be a short piece with limited information but it means a whole lot more to me, I can assure you. And it is another loose end dealt with, to boot.

Further information came to me on Sunday evening, the 12th June 2022 while watching the film Titanic, again!

I thought I had done the SR for dad a while ago but

to my surprise there was work still to do.

During the Titanic SR my teammates and I had succeeded in general but for dad, all we were to do was bring his soul up from the seabed to connect with me where he has stayed well hidden until now, almost 3 years on. He has been waiting patiently for mum's soul from this lifetime to arrive, so they could leave together, mum having passed later in life. I have no idea how long the trapped part of mum's soul has been with me but she and dad made themselves clearly felt during the film. Leaving me in no uncertain terms there was work to do. The reuniting of mum and dad's soul from Titanic now complete and boy what a truly amazing feeling I felt when they finally came together, a wave of pure love encompassing the whole of my body, It was definitely a true love connection. No wonder I was stopped from doing work on this book over the weekend and when seeing where I had left off, well you'd never guess but I had stopped reading at this particular SR. Wow amazing, SR definitely completed, fingers crossed.

Part 2

The New SRs

The Tower Block SR ~ 14th December 2020

THIS SR IS being included because of its slight difference in experience for me. I only realised after the SR had been completed the enormity of what we, my SR teammates and I had achieved.

Pat, a lovely lady and friend, had contacted me about doing a SR and an EC at her home, which was the top floor of a block of flats three stories high.

On the morning of 14th December I arrived at Pat's and went through the process of chatting, firstly to see what was going on and then going from room to room to see if there were any slight differences in the room temperature or signs that this flat was indeed housing trapped souls. And as soon as I arrived I asked my SR teammates to place a circle of light around the whole building, which constituted around twelve to fifteen flats.

I thought no more of this until things started to get a bit confusing. Pat told me a few things she could sense in her flat, but she also told me about a man who had passed away in the flat below and other various happenings.

If we look at this (or any other) block of flats we will notice that there will be a vast amount of emotional and mental energy dispensed from each flat. Each person in those flats will have trapped parts of their souls with them awaiting such a time as this. This situation will go back to the first inhabitants of these flats when they were first built. Similarly, if we include whoever had ever died on the land this block of flats was built on, we will realise that we will be doing the SR for them too.

When I went into the bedroom I felt a presence, which Pat had already told me about. But then I started to feel other energies. These were trapped souls, but they didn't tally with what Pat had told me about her flat.

It took a few moments, but then the penny dropped. My SR teammates had placed a circle of light around the whole block of flats, and this was an open invitation to the souls trapped in the other flats as well.

I was picking up the souls who had resided in the flats below as they rose into the light to move on.

Pat had only called me to do work on her flat, when in truth she had been the conduit to help all the souls in the block of flats.

The SR took a little while longer than usual. But with the number of souls being given the opportunity to move on, that is quite understandable.

The Impregnable Fortress SR ~ 12th to 15th March 2021

THIS SPECIFIC SR crept up on me very slowly and subtly, with a lot of denial from me over the years. But now I know why.

A few weeks before this came up I had been to the chippy for some dinner with Debbie, who then drove past a particular house, no. 158 Oxford Street, which was my former home. I became quite annoyed as we went past, but obviously this happened to bring my emotions up and to help initiate this SR. So thank you, Debbie.

Ever since Dad helped to remove me from my home in 2015, I have at times asked myself, 'Do I need to move back into no. 158?' It was my former home for fifty years.

Now I have mentioned this situation in previous SRs. However, this SR is the final time you will hear about it.

You may recall my mentioning that in 1999 a situation occurred where I ended up in hospital with a broken cheekbone and damaged knee ligaments, which all resulted from a very unpleasant experience.

I allowed myself to be drawn into a fight. The circumstances through this day created it as it was meant to be, but I have only just realised why.

There is no need to go into all the details regarding how I ended up in hospital. The main issue is what happened during this distressing experience.

Once I had been kicked unconscious, the right circumstances were created so that the existing soul in me, which had resided within my body from birth, was able to leave. Then another soul, Shanti, was able to move in. All this had to happen during the time I was unconscious.

More amazing still is the fact that a part of the soul who left only partially left. This means that part of this soul remained with me, trapped. I did not know this until a few days ago.

The information came in dribs and drabs, as it seems to in most of the SRs I do. I sense that it happens this way so that I will refrain from trying to force any information through which may not be completely true. This teaches me patience and teaches me to trust in the process.

The information started to flow in via the visions of experiences I have had when I have been away and have thought that the only place where I would be able to buy the items of clothing that I needed would be from the town I lived in, Leigh. This is strange, I know, but one example of this belief came while I was in Whitby.

I needed a new pair of jeans. The first place I thought of was Leigh Market so I rang them, but there was no answer.

I did end up ordering some jeans off the Internet. But the whole thing was so strange. My thought process since leaving my home in 2015 has always been that I need to buy clothes or anything substantial from Leigh, as if there was no other place that sold clothes or anything else I needed. Doubly strange.

As I have said earlier, a few times I've asked myself, 'Do I need to move back into our previous home in Oxford Street?' Now, knowing that I had no need to do this, but feeling a presence telling me otherwise, would really bring up a feeling of fear within me.

I need to go back into our experiences as a family for a moment. Mum and Dad had my brother Jack before I was born but he only lived for twenty-four hours. So while I – as we all are – was born through the love vibration, my body, while within the womb, was being bombarded with negative energies from both Mum and Dad.

The emotions they felt I can only guess at – like fear, sadness, guilt, anger, despair and heartbreak. I am sure you can think of others too.

Dad turned his emotions inwards. He effectively shut his heart down for fear of it breaking again, while Mum doted on me, spoiling me greatly at every opportunity. Both Mum and Dad dealt with their emotions the best way they could.

Now, during this time, my physical body was taking on more and more negativity from both my parents, which is only natural, and this affected me in the way I felt. I have been shown various times in my childhood where I saw my home not just as a home but as an impregnable fortress. When I got inside I was safe, and no one could hurt me.

This obviously carried on throughout my adult life, to the moment of the soul exchange, when Shanti took over the reins.

Yet, with the trapped soul from the first part of my life, all these experiences emotions and memories were still embedded within my physical body for me to work through heal and release.

So now having this information things started to come together as a jigsaw does. Each time I made it back to my impregnable fortress I was relying more and more on this solid and dependable building as my protector.

Over a period of fifty years this became an immensely powerful attachment indeed. It was so powerful that, during my time as carer for Dad, the time came for him to instigate a very extreme situation to help me break free of this attachment.

I have written about the fact that Dad had come at me with a knife previously. This action ended up with me losing my home, my job and my dad all within a few hours. After this happened, I only got to see him once for five minutes before he passed.

However, everything Dad did in those moments before and after the attack I now see as a true blessing. Dad not only saved me from experiencing even more trauma, had I stayed in the house as his carer and his son, but he also acted in a way that helped me begin to break this immensely powerful attachment to our home. It really did take all this unpleasantness to help me successfully break the cord of this attachment, five years after Dad's initial godlike act.

After having received all the pieces of the jigsaw, on

the 14th March I began to do the work necessary to help this part of my previous soul move on. I had now accepted and released all the emotions attached to this trapped soul.

Oh, the 14th March, just happens to be Mum and Dad's wedding anniversary... Is this a coincidence? Not a chance.

This is how God/Goddess and our angels work – so magically, if sometimes very mysteriously. I instigated the SR, which ended at Rivington, in the same spot where I have carried out a few SRs in the past. We must be building some sort of energetic portal there. It seems that it's a place where souls choose to take their next step on their everlasting journey. It is a beautiful spot.

There are moments in life that alter our direction in extreme ways. This is one of those times, but in a most positive way. I am so grateful to Dad for his selfless, unconditionally loving actions.

I know it is all hypothetical now, but had he not done what he did... Well, who knows where both he and I would be now?

Like I say, it's all irrelevant now, but thank you, Dad. I love you so much.

The Happy SR ~ from 2011 to 3rd May 2021

This SR began in the healing room at Yvonne's, where I was told of a lifetime in which my soul was very happy. The vision Yvonne relayed to me sounded blissful. My physical body in that lifetime was walking along an avenue lined with trees. The sun was shining, and everything in my world was good. The time was around the 1890s in London. I was wearing a top hat and carried a walking cane. I was clearly quite a well-to-do gentleman.

While in this state of bliss, I had no idea that I had passed on. However, the conclusion of this SR didn't occur during the healing. But it did reconnect that part of my soul to me. For over ten years it had silently been waiting for the moment it was to make itself known to me, which, funnily enough, was the day before Mum's birthday, 2nd May 2021.

Now this lifetime was shared with a soul who I have had many experiences with. The lady involved will remain nameless in this instance.

SRs that involve happy times can be the toughest nuts to crack in terms of the soul wanting to move on –

simply because of the fear of not believing that they will experience another lifetime such as the one they have just experienced, which is understandable.

This part of my soul was hindering me like this: until now I hadn't been aware of it or had been able to detach myself from the happy emotions that were limiting me with regard to being open for a relationship in this life at this time. This makes sense to me because I know that there is a beautiful lady waiting to enter my life. But until I clear all the issues surrounding any number of past-life experiences this lady will feel energetically that I'm not ready to give the relationship a hundred per cent.

However, as I now believe that there is a lifetime, a moment, a relationship that will eclipse even the happiest lifetimes long gone, I have had to do the necessary work to pave the way for such a relationship. It does show how my soul's journey and its lessons have affected each lifetime until it had cleared the decks mentally and emotionally so to speak. This is just one experience that had to wait.

Everything is in divine and perfect order. It really is.

So on 2nd May 2021 I was made aware that this part of my soul was with me via the odd bit of noise, and was able to conclude the SR that night and throughout the next day on Mum's birthday after being guided to the special place up at Rivington, where that part of my soul was met by the lady in the happy lifetime.

Both went up into the light hand in hand. Beautiful. Quite emotional, too. There are much better times ahead for me, as there surely are for you.

The Dementia SR ~
13th May 2021 to 19th May 2021

THIS SR HAS also crept up on me subtly, with hints of great amazement.

I woke on the Thursday morning with the thought that I must visit a recently found crystal shop in Chorley called Crystal Aura.

I had no idea why I was to visit this shop. I just knew I needed to, for some reason.

At the shop, while talking to Jaime the owner, we spoke about various topics, which led to Jaime telling me that a lady had spent a very long time in her shop the day before, holding on to one specific crystal.

Jaime told me that the lady seemed a little vulnerable and that she had another lady with her, who seemed to be the lady's carer. Jaime also told me, as the lady was leaving, that she had expressed how different she felt – lighter – in a positive way.

Our conversation ended. I went about my day and started to experience alarming experiences, for example:

1. I could be doing something and then completely forget what I was doing or where I was.

2. I felt very unstable and unsure of myself, which was strange.
3. I seemed to be drifting from one realm to another with ease, but it was so disconcerting at the same time.

These and other experiences continued throughout the evening.

When I woke the following morning I was greeted by the trapped soul of a lady, who in a matter of minutes told me that she had connected to me at the crystal shop the day before.

She had spent the time in the shop holding the crystal and had allowed this trapped part of her soul to embed itself into the crystal until I arrived.

I found myself talking very slowly and very gently to this lady, obviously knowing she was ready to move on, but having no idea how she became trapped in the first place.

Then I went to Rivington and continued to speak gently to the lady, who I now knew to be called Nancy.

We arrived at my special SR place, where I have done many SRs in the past, and began the SR in earnest. Nancy moved on very swiftly indeed.

Now here is where it gets interesting.

On my way back to the car I got a vision of the word *dementia*, which was somehow connected to Dad and his state when he passed.

Only now do I realise it was Dad who brought this word to my attention.

It transpires that Nancy had passed with dementia

and that Dad had imprinted on me some of his symptoms while alive so that I was able to experience what it was like to have dementia, albeit very briefly.

This blew me away. It certainly explained all the strange and unpleasant goings-on the previous evening.

I trusted what I received. It was not easy, if I am honest, but trust it I did.

I was, however, blessed with confirmation of everything that I felt during a healing session with Yvonne on Tuesday 18th May.

Even more humbling was the fact that this SR had connected me to the vibration of so many souls who have passed due to dementia and dementia-type issues, and so I was now blessed with the tools to help these trapped souls.

Dad had blessed me with a glimpse, however brief, of what it was like to experience a type of dementia.

I know it was a very gentle version of this illness. But it gifted me with such a passion to help these souls even more than the souls who become trapped in other ways, because this way of passing really is the nearest thing to what I would call hell.

I use Dad's state during his dementia and how I viewed him and his mood changes, which could happen at the drop of a hat.

I came to understand that when Dad was at peace and had a smile on his face he was in another world, literally.

When he was frustrated and angry, he was back on Planet Earth or in another less pleasant world.

He was constantly flipping from one world to another even at the time when he passed.

I must have done the work to help Dad to move on from this experience during the SRs I have done for him.

However, it shows how these souls are truly stranded in limbo.

It is a true gift and an honour for me to be able help those souls who have passed with dementia move on now, for there are a great many around the world at this time who have passed with this type of illness.

Let me state categorically that I would rather there were no period of time when a soul is trapped.

However, due to the journeys of our souls, many have fallen foul of this most unpleasant illness. So if I can do my bit and play my part in helping set them free from their state of limbo I am so blessed to do so, with the help of all my SR friends. What an amazing experience. Thank you, God, for these blessed gifts.

The morning of 4th March 2022.

I feel duty-bound to add my experience this morning, for it shows how subtly I have honed my spiritual senses over a ten-month period, with immense and priceless help from my angelic friends. The above-mentioned SR took days to complete. Yet this morning it took just thirty minutes from the initial contact with my neighbour to a very swift end. The synchronicity of this morning has been truly highlighted for me.

I seemed to be taking forever to get ready to set off into Bolton. Eventually, when I did, it was perfectly timed because when driving past the bus stop I saw a neighbour waiting, so I stopped and offered him a lift.

He was in the car for about five minutes at most, but this was more than enough time for a part of his wife's soul to leap from him to me.

By the time I had parked my car and headed to the bank I started to feel a little lost. This was highlighted by the fact that I had to go back into the bank because I thought I had lost the ticket for the car park. This was after looking through the cards in my wallet and not seeing the ticket wedged between them.

When I had returned to my car and sitting in the driver's seat I said to my angels that this short trip had been a very surreal one.

At the very same moment, a message came through via a picture of some rose oil that I had ordered a week or so ago. This was a sign that I needed to go and pick it up, so off I went.

Moments after setting off, I began to sense there was a trapped soul with me. I thought it was the soul of a gentlemen I had given a lift to at first, so went with it. As I spoke to him I sensed that this soul had passed with dementia-type issues, so I spoke gently and repeated much of what I said with even more empathy and patience. I invited my SR friends to be with me and to instigate a SR at that very moment while we drove to Leyland, about thirty minutes away.

By the time I had arrived at Leyland the SR had been completed. I had understood that it was the trapped soul of the gentleman's wife who had passed with the issues and, more importantly, had been made aware that the emotions and healing connected with this type of SR can be released as easily as any other SR.

I then entered the crystal shop and was blessed with

the sweetest-smelling rose oil I have ever smelt. I was also blessed with a sageing down, to free myself from any residual emotions or feelings from this beautiful soul.

The amazing thing is that I was aware of the subtle energies much sooner than I had been in the past and was thus able to help the soul move on more quickly, without experiencing many of the emotions and feelings she passed with.

I feel so blessed to have attained a level of experience, sensitivity and connectivity to my angelic friends and to my own inner knowing. This has helped me delve deeper into my life's calling, and I am now able to do this work with even more passion and focus. I love every second of it.

It's a win–win situation for all concerned. Thank you, angels.

Further magical insight came to me on 15th March 2022

This was an extension of the information I have already received, and it was connected to dementia and other related issues.

This time I was shown and experienced someone who had passed with the slightly different symptoms of Alzheimer's. During that morning I felt a little confused and was unable to process the simplest of the actions I was trying to complete. Doubt was also prominent in my mind but it was present in a much subtler way than the experience of dementia through Dad and during other SRs I have done for those passing with dementia.

This experience has spanned four days, so I do take this as my initiation into being able to discern from those who pass with dementia and those who pass from Alzheimer's and other related issues. I'm not sure what the difference is, nor why I'm adding this piece, but I do trust my guides. So if they deem it to be important information, who am I to argue?

Indeed, I'm sure I will be blessed with further information that will perfectly outline the very subtle differences of these issues and how to go about doing a SR for each one in a unique way that's best suited for them. I will also make sure that they are catered for in every way as they are lovingly helped to move on from this most unpleasant of experiences.

The souls that are trapped in whatever way are priority, first, second and last.

The lady whose soul had connected with me has now thankfully left for pastures new and has left me with another priceless experience, which I can now add to my spiritual toolkit.

Thank you, angels.

A Mother and Father Dementia
SR ~ 20th & 21st May 2021

NO SOONER HAD I received confirmation via my angelic friends of this new gift than I was called into service very swiftly indeed. It was instigated via a chat with a friend, who told me about a specific person (who shall remain nameless) whose parents had both passed with dementia.

This small piece of information brought into alignment so much regarding this lady's ongoing challenging experiences. The lady in question had never mentioned this fact to me. But now here I was being told this information realising that this issue was her main problem, which was sorely in need of attention. Talk about divine timing.

It was primarily for her to seek further help from me, and after she had asked for help I could then allow myself to express what I knew about her situation. And, with her impending request for further healing, I would be able to bring this amazing SR to a wonderful conclusion for the lady and for her parents too.

Last night the lady asked for further help. As we talked, her mother then her father made themselves known to me via an energy surge around me.

It is not for me to tell people what I know or what I can do to help them. It's for those people – perhaps you – to ask for my help. Only then can I share the information with them or you. Otherwise it would seem as if I were trying to coax them into having a healing. This is not the way of the healer or the soul retriever. It must be the person's choice to ask or not, so that they keep the power of choice regarding their situation. They may not be ready for the healing or the SR work. So until they do ask, it's for me to keep mum. And to always respect their choices. This includes you too, my friend.

The lady had carried these two trapped souls with her since they both passed, around seventeen years ago. No wonder she was experiencing a particularly challenging life.

As I have come to understand, when any part of our soul has become trapped in whatever way, we become the vessel that can release all the emotions from that lifetime. For this lady it was a real challenge to release all these emotions for her mother and father, who had both passed with dementia. All I can say is that she took on an immense job and, more importantly, succeeded in bringing it to completion.

The lady asked me to do what I could to bring this situation to a close for all their sakes, which I and my SR teammates most assuredly did.

Through my noticeably short dalliance with experiencing the very unpleasant symptoms of dementia, I was now able to fully comprehend and empathise regarding how much this lady had carried with her for over twenty years (she had cared for her parents before their passing). Now I know which burdens she has had to carry, my respect for the lady in question has risen markedly.

The SR started last night and brought some incredible insight. The mother and father obviously passed at different times, so ended up in different realities. They were in the same house, searching for each other but always unable to connect, until the moment when I realised that they had come together via me as the conduit. They were now finally back together and very swiftly left as they ascended a beautiful flight of white marble stairs leading to heaven, hand in hand.

My SR friends had conjured up the most perfect scene to help these angels move on in the easiest way possible.

The Brucie Bonus from this experience is that it has helped the lady really believe that her parents did love each other. Now that alone is magical.

That was it. The SR was completed. It was very intense but amazing to be a part of this SR team.

I am so blessed.

On a personal level I have been blessed with additional information regarding how Dad shared the part of his soul with me and when.

The transference began when Dad, having just passed on the morning of Friday 5th February 2016 around 3 20 a.m., visited me in what I believed to be a dream state. Dad came in and kissed me as if to say, 'I love you, son,' which was lovely.

However, later that morning I found out he had passed, so I rushed round to our home to see him and to begin the process, as is necessary during a death.

Dad's gift to me as he left for another realm was to leave part of his soul (trapped) which housed the experiences he had had during his spell with dementia and various other emotions for me to connect with while clearing the house for sale. This took four months to complete.

This part of dad's soul lay dormant until the morning when I woke feeling I needed to visit the crystal shop in the previous SR experience. The activation commenced, and the rest is history.

I have been to Rivington today (21st May 2022) to finalise a SR to release any unhealthy connections to Dad through this situation.

This was completed without tears. I felt a great weight lift from my shoulders. Though I was shown nothing of the SR, I knew that everything had been done to tie up all the loose ends.

Dementia: Additional Information ~ 18th & 19th June 2021

I HAVE BEEN receiving a steady inflow of information regarding dementia, Alzheimer's and related issues and what some of the spiritual issues are behind these ailments through SRs I have done recently.

I received this short message... *Dementia is in part created via a fear or resistance to all things spiritual, the awakening process and the fear of the unknown; not wanting to face the unpleasant experiences we have had.*

When we ignore or resist the opportunities to awaken, we compound the situation in a truly negative way. Indecisiveness is another symptom that I believe can add to dementia and to dementia-related issues too. Our mind becomes overloaded with unpleasant thoughts, visions and memories from the past that become too many to cope with. The more that these thoughts, visions and memories come to us, the more confusing the experience. It causes a deeper feeling of vulnerability, which in turn leads to a more unpleasant experience of the state of dementia and related issues. We then start to bury them deep within, blocking them as if they never happened, rather than facing them. This is what I believe to be the core of the matter within dementia and related issues.

Learning to quieten our mind can help calm the confusion via SR and EC work, natural healing techniques, meditation and being in nature. But, more importantly, when these issues surface we must accept them, face them and do the healing work necessary so that the build-up is never too much for us to cope with.

Below is an example using a pinball machine that my SR guides gave me to explain people experiencing dementia at different levels. Each person experiencing these issues will experience them in a unique way, with perhaps slightly different symptoms!

As you know, a pinball normally pings gently to and fro from one pin to another, but sometimes if the ball gets wedged between two very close pins it can ping very quickly from one to another. I feel that this explains the extremes of these issues perfectly. I also believe that this is how dementia and related issues are experienced by a person moving from dimension to dimension at various speeds. No wonder that it can be a very disconcerting and harrowing experience for those with these related issues.

These bouts can come on at any time and for a prolonged period, which makes them worse in some ways. Again, I believe this can create a state of anticipatory fear of when and if they begin again, thus adding to the person's already increasingly poor mental and emotional state.

The gift I have been blessed with, I honestly believe, through my divine calling as a soul retriever, can now be helped via SR if a loved one's trapped soul attaches to them. And now I also understand the problems presented by people whose ancestors have been through this same issue or any other type of ailment or issue but who are unable to do the spiritual work necessary to clear it.

Helping the trapped soul move on helps remove the symptoms and the feelings that can become a real part of our own well-being. We can so easily be taking on our ancestors' issues without even knowing it, as I have experienced at first hand. Doing the work necessary – helping to break the cycle created by our ancestors, connected to dementia or any other ailment, for that matter – creates a win–win situation for all.

I do believe that dementia, as with all other ailments and issues, is passed on by our ancestors. We at this time have an opportunity to release these issues through our physical bodies. This is not easy, but it may well be what our soul has chosen to experience.

It may be worth revisiting the piece called *Hereditary* that I wrote in *Taxi for 'Spirit' - Diary of a Soul Retriever*.

Here is a short example of and a reminder of hereditary issues:

Just as a stroke, a heart attack, angina and any other heart-related issues are connected to a heart becoming closed, these unpleasant experiences can come to open our heart to greater love when they are meant to. This is the same with any unresolved ancestral issues.

My ancestors' hereditary heart issue:
I know this goes back through generations of my ancestors. My granddad had angina. He was a man of very few words, as was Dad. They would bottle things up but were very sensitive souls. They also harboured a fear of loss and were unable to express their feelings. This caused them to create a wall of protection around their hearts, which gradually became thicker with each loss they experienced, especially when it came to loved ones and close friends.

For Dad, Granddad and further back on along my Dad's family line this issue grows stronger as each generation fails to deal with the issues pertaining to the heart (or whatever the issue may be).

Granddad had angina and passed away from a stroke, and probably dementia too. Dad however had heightened, more unpleasant issues with his heart. He had three heart attacks in quick succession, a triple heart bypass and angina, which led to his stroke.

Now, had I not taken the panic attack I had in 2003 seriously, I know I would have experienced even more issues with the heart, for I too would have been resisting and denying the fact that these issues existed. Thankfully I accepted the wake-up call and followed the guidance to where I am now fully on my spiritual path.

Through the strength and support I have received from many beloved ancestors and angels I have been able to change our ancestors' direction, helping them heal in the process.

Each strand of golden thread that I have rewoven into our family's ancestral tapestry lifts its heaviness and creates new health and wellness. I have faced the issues my ancestors were unable to in their lifetime. A new and better future beckons for us all. I believe, due to the healing I have done on my own heart, that I have released the emotions connected to any ancestral issues, some of which have been painful and unpleasant. However, it is much better to face these issues than to ignore them.

After seeking alternative help through much reiki and other forms of natural healing, and vast amounts of support from friends who are also on a spiritual path, I have brought this cycle for my ancestors to an end.

I thank each one of them, for they now walk with me, supporting me as I move forward on my path. In time I will have recreated a new tapestry for my ancestors, full of light and love. All the heaviness and pain will soon be no more.

I have come to believe for perhaps almost every soul who passes with some form of dementia or Alzheimer's that a part of their soul is most likely to become trapped, due to them fluctuating from dimension to dimension while in a physical body.

In no way am I touting for work. I have no need to compete. Therefore I share my knowledge so that others may pursue their calling, which may well include SR. We are here to help each other. So, through these divinely guided words, if I can help those with dementia or any other related ailments, I am only too glad to share or help.

People or trapped souls who connect with me for a

SR will do so because of a prearranged agreement, a soul contract that had already been written while sitting in God's waiting room before coming to earth.

An example of a trapped soul attaching to a close loved one when passing from dementia occurred when I was at a friend's mum's having a meal. I was talking to her mum's partner when he told me that his brother had passed just days earlier.

I felt straight away that a part of his brother's soul had attached to him. And even though it was in the infancy of this attachment it was affecting his health, albeit ever so slightly.

If this gentleman were to leave this matter unattended he would undoubtedly take on those symptoms of dementia at a deeper level.

It is not for me to tell this person (or indeed anyone else) what I can sense, feel or know to be true. I must be approached and asked for help before sharing my knowledge in this way. I must abide by the spiritual laws.

This law is all about keeping the on right side of the boundary. If I were to step over the boundary and share my knowledge by forcing it upon anyone, however pure and good my intentions were, this would create karma for me and would be of no help to those who I forced my beliefs upon. Stepping over the spiritual boundary is extremely hard to not do at times. I can only hope that somewhere in the future this gentleman and his family may come to seek my counsel. Only then will I be able to express my truth in full.

Here is an update...

In December 2021 I met the gentleman at the same venue. This time his brother's soul was ready to move on. I was guided to do a SR but, after I began to feel unwell, I went to the toilet and while there I asked my guides what was going on? Once I understood I then instigated a SR while in the bathroom, within minutes the trapped soul of the gentleman's brother had moved on.

This SR was again a soul contract we had agreed upon that I and my SR teammates would come back to bring closure to.

Trinity's Baptism into SR ~ May 2021 to 24th June 2021

During the period of lockdown around March 2021, and in conjunction with Jaime opening her first crystal shop, Trinity, Jaime's daughter, began to experience what it is like to have a trapped soul connect with her.

However, like more and more people will experience in the future, she had no idea what to do until we met.

Trinity would have had very subtle hints from the trapped soul in the beginning and would have known little about his attempts to get her attention, but over the last few months the soul has ramped up his efforts to make Trinity very aware that he was ready to move on.

However, when hearing of Trinity's experiences, I soon understood that he was unable to move on, for he sought forgiveness from Trinity and her soul regarding a past-life experience they had shared, an unpleasant one.

After an informal chat with Jaime she then in turn spoke to Trinity and intimated that she may benefit by asking for my help. She also asked if I would do a SR to help move this gentleman on. His antics had become quite extreme when trying to get Trinity's attention. Trinity did ask for my help when I called into the shop minutes later... Divine timing or what?

This is how trapped souls communicate. They cannot physically speak, so how do you get someone's attention? Easy. You make as much noise as possible, which this gentleman certainly did.

Trinity told me that over a short period of time a selenite crystal fell to the floor of its own accord, a dish of crystals experienced the same fate, which caused some damage, a dragon ornament moved horizontally across the shop and a dreamcatcher unhooked itself from the ceiling and fell to the ground.

But the most amazing occurrence for me, and the one with the biggest message, happened only a few days ago. Five copies of my book *Taxi for 'Spirit'* fell from an upright position on to the shelf, causing other items to fall to the floor.

Now to have my books in the shop on sale was perfect for the soul to get his point over very subtly, but succinctly too. With Trinity's knowledge of SR expanding she knew that this was a definite sign, but only realised that this was the case when I told her why the books were used in this way. It was a cryptic sign to call on me to come and do a SR.

It is easy for me to see these signs but, as it was with Trinity and perhaps with you, it will be a challenge in the beginning. However, through these books I know you will become more aware of any strange occurrences within your home and act on them accordingly.

The other thing to look out for, as with Trinity, is this. When these inexplicable occurrences happen, if they happen when you are on your own this is a sign that the trapped soul is directly connected to a lifetime experience with your soul. And however extreme these experiences become, please know that the trapped soul is not trying to hurt anyone. They are simply seeking help so they can move on.

If these signs are ignored the experiences will be ramped up by the soul until they are understood and action is taken.

I may have said this before... I do not believe in a place called hell, but a trapped soul imprisoned within an unpleasant past-life experience is the closest thing I would term as being in hell. If you can imagine an unpleasant ending to life, then understand hypothetically that if a part of your soul becomes trapped it becomes trapped in the series of experiences leading up to the physical body passing. It is then stuck in this seemingly never-ending Groundhog Day, experiencing these very limited and unpleasant experiences over and over until someone can help it move on. This is why I feel so privileged and honoured to help these souls.

So I spoke to Trinity on Tuesday the 22nd June and arranged to visit the shop and do a SR at her request. The book experience happened yesterday, on 23rd June. I feel the soul was making sure we had heard him, as we had already arranged to do a SR.

Today, the 24th June, I arrived at 10 a.m., following my guidance, which included me inviting Trinity to say a few words to the gentleman's soul.

This is what he was waiting for. As Trinity spoke sincerely, forgiving him, she felt a weight lift from her shoulders, which was a sign that the gentleman had finally let go and moved on. Amazing.

The Ostracised SR ~ 24th & 25th June 2021

THIS SR HAS been an amazing series of events. I did the above SR for Trinity, then visited the crystal shop in Leyland. While talking to Jaime we spoke about the man who had hanged himself in the flat above the shop in Chorley. As Jaime talked about the man she experienced an assortment of energies, which signified to me that the man had attached himself to her.

The man then made his presence known to me. I became aware of this when I also experienced differing energies around me. I did not fully understand what had occurred during our chat until this morning, when I felt guided to do a SR for the man in question, who had obviously attached himself to me.

I followed my intuition and felt that the man had moved on after I had explained certain things to him. But, as I was to find out only hours later, he had not moved on. And for what I was gifted later in the day I am truly thankful that he stayed with me for those few extra hours.

Jaime had experienced a few disturbing noises during their tenancy of the shop and at one point had to go upstairs into the flat above for some reason. This is where I now believe the man attached himself to Jamie, knowing that she was the best option for him to get help to move on.

The lady who lives in the flat was obviously not ready to deal with a trapped soul. However, I do believe that the man was connected to her soul. Most of the experiences and noises emanated from the flat as he was trying to get the lady's attention. When he was unable to, he changed tactics and attached himself to Jaime.

So here I am again at Rivington, the scene of many a SR, preparing for a SR I did not really want to do. And with good cause, for it brought up some really deep core emotions that I had hidden deep down inside.

Just as I was to begin the SR I heard many rapid loud bangs in the near distance that sounded like guns going off. This brought to my attention how it would feel on a battlefield in WWI. This was the information that came through, so I trusted it accordingly.

It then led me to realise this man had been in the war and had endured many unpleasant experiences. As I went further into the SR, I got the words court martial.

I found out that the man had refused to act on an order given by a superior officer, which had led to him being court-martialled. This man had obviously put up with as much as he could and had felt that he could do no more harm to others, regardless of what side they were on. It was a brave step to take, but one his soul would have been overjoyed with.

Now the man had no idea what his actions would set in motion further on in his life. It was no bed of roses for him, that is for sure. His comrades in the forces turned on him and his family castigated him and disowned him, which led to a life of misery, regret and loneliness, even though he did have the odd friend.

Living like this took its toll on this man. He was unable to take any more, so in an act of desperation he hanged himself.

When this information came to me, I told him how proud I was of him and of the way he stood up for himself against the authorities because of his beliefs. I said his soul was so proud of his stance, and indeed the angels in heaven applauded his strength too.

To take a stand as this man did took great courage, strength and faith, but here is the thing. His experience awoke within me a similar situation, where I had stood my ground for my new-found beliefs regarding my spiritual path.

My friends at the time said little, but I knew they did not understand my new path. Two of them were very vocal in making their point perfectly clearly in their discontent regarding my beliefs. Both had me in tears. One stated that I needed to seek counselling. The other savagely ripped into my books, saying they would never amount to anything and that everything I was putting on my Facebook page via angel posts and uplifting posts was, for want of a better word, daft.

So I was able to empathise with the man who stood up for his beliefs. It took some guts for both the man and for me (and indeed for anyone who goes against the grain) to do what we did. It takes real strength for anyone to stand up for beliefs that very few others understand.

When realising how hard it had been for me initially

on my path, I let go a few tears and released a weight off my shoulders too. It was a burden I had carried for a long time. The man had too.

It was a massive release for both of us when the man finally accepted the support of my angelic SR friends who were helping him move on.

This experience was the forerunner of an even deeper issue with me. It brought up the lack of forgiveness I was still harbouring towards two very dear friends, one a human angel and one an angel in spirit. All this revolved around Dad's passing.

I had had a healing with Yvonne a few days before Dad passed. Both Yvonne and Archangel Michael knew Dad was going to pass very soon but did not tell me during the healing.

Now I have done work on this issue a few times, going deeper each time, but this surprised me a little when it came to my attention.

Within moments I found myself talking to my inner child, who through a healing in December of last year had been brought back into alignment. This was affecting the healing process of my inner child. Since this amazing healing I have been taken back into issues I thought I had dealt with – only to find that now, as my inner child had finally been brought back into alignment, he was now able to heal, release and let go of the emotions he was unable to before.

This was another of those inner child issues. I have known for a while that had Yvonne and Archangel Michael told me this information I would have undoubtedly tried to get to be with Dad as he passed. Had I been successful, Dad and I would have had to come back into another lifetime and go through much of what we had gone through in this life. Me being with Dad at the moment of his passing would have kept many cycles unfinished.

I was always meant to be absent at Dad's passing. Dad said through Yvonne at a healing (afternoon) on the same day as his funeral (morning) that had I been with him he would have found it hard to move on. He needed to be alone, physically alone (I know that Mum, Jack and many ancestors and angels were with him, helping his transition). Around the same time as Dad passed I had a dream experience, where Dad came and kissed me on the cheek.

I did not realise what this meant until I got a message later that morning saying that Dad had passed. When I got the message and went home and into the house, I first saw the table set for three places. Very intense emotions poured out because I believed Dad knew it was time and he was leaving me a message. It broke my heart, and how. He had, over a period of time, started to pack his suitcases. I firmly believe that he was making it easier for me to clear his things out when he passed.

I then went upstairs and saw Dad lying on the floor.

I will not go into further details, but will just say this: in the bathroom the clock had stopped at 3.20 a.m. I honestly believe this was the time Dad moved-on. It is still bringing emotion up as I type. I love you, Dad.

Dad, upon his physical body shutting down, did visit

me on his way back to the light. He was saying goodbye for now.

Did I anticipate or expect any of these amazing insights and experiences to unfold like they have today? The answer is a resounding 'No.' But boy, how grateful I am. These experiences really are priceless.

> Thank you, angels, one and all.

This is a prime example of how with a series of issues each step brings up deeper emotions, if we follow the guidance given, as they finally lead to the core issue. This for me was the loss of Dad, and the feeling that I had failed Dad in my desire to be with him at the end. He shed lots of the emotion he had held within him during the years since his stroke. Another win–win situation.

I do love my job and my calling.

I simply had to add this to this divinely created book.

The Reptilian Race SRs ~ 16th June 2021 to 9th August 2021

THIS LATEST SR began in the beautiful surroundings of Yvonne's healing room, during which Archangel Metatron placed me in his Merkabah cube and proceeded to take me through the universe and beyond to collate parts of my soul that were trapped in other dimensions and worlds. This occurred during the actual healing part of the session with Yvonne, while I relaxed on the bed.

We now jump forward to today, 9th July. My mind was at odds with a situation I knew I had to face. But boy, did I have a challenge to see it through.

Before Archangel Metatron's blessed gift I had never even given a moment's thought to the possibility that our souls could be trapped in other worlds.

Now I know that this was all part of the plan, a magical step that my angelic friends had created, in order to bring about such an amazing experience and a SR this very evening. The situation involved a chat and a compromise to be reached, which suited both parties, and in a way I had never thought of.

This SR is part of the deal that I and the other person involved made.

At one point in the conversation a ladybird landed on this person's hand. When the conversation ended I saw the ladybird in my window. I put my finger on the window to offer it as a mode of transport out of the house, which the ladybird duly took advantage of.

Outside the person saw the ladybird and proceeded to place it back onto their hand. I took this as a confirmation of what I was getting through my thoughts, regarding what needed to be done and who to call upon for this amazing SR.

This very brief connection between my finger and the person's hand was enough for a soul to attach themselves to me. I was unaware of this at the time. As the day wore on I became increasingly frustrated, to the point when I tried to swat a fly that had obviously signed up to be a focal point but had triggered my frustration instead by continuously landing on me. This was also part of the plan.

This, I have come to understand, was the emotions or feelings from the soul who connected with me. I am becoming more sensitive to these energies and signs. Yet another divine gift.

By mid-evening I began to feel a build-up of the various energies of the angels and the soul who had connected with me earlier. This was my sign to set the final steps in motion to help this soul move on, but to also help him understand what had led him to be in this precarious situation.

Oh, by the way, this soul was a reptilian from another world.

At the time of writing about this SR the world is going through a great many changes, one of which is the eradication of off-world dark beings, such as reptilians, who have over thousands of years created a world of unpleasantness and chaos. This is all I am willing to say currently. You will undoubtedly read and hear about the goings-on in this world very soon indeed.

This soul had infiltrated the physical body of the person who I had the conversation with without being invited, like a cuckoo taking over another bird's nest. This person had had a fearful experience in the past that had created an opening, a dip in vibration. This was the opportunity for the reptilian to step in and take over the running of their physical body, causing mayhem in the process.

> Please notice I use the word *soul* and not the words *trapped soul*...

This SR has been so different from the ones I have been blessed to do previously. There are two parts to this SR. The first part is to empathetically explain to the reptilian how his actions had caused a great deal of unpleasantness for many.

However, as I spoke to him, in a clear and concise manner, channelling what I needed to express to this beautiful soul... Yes, you read that right. I spoke to this soul as I would any other soul, trapped or otherwise, for we are all connected, and whatever this soul had caused others to experience our souls have had similar experiences too...

I have, very recently (March 2022) been gifted more information about our reptilian friends and the various types of reptilians, some, perhaps all are unable to hear our words but do feel them vibrationally. There is more information to be shared in the future but this needed to be aired here for you now.

As I spoke to this beautiful soul I began to see similarities between his journey and my soul Shanti's journey.

Let me elaborate. My soul Shanti has had many life experiences on earth. Some have caused others to experience unpleasantness and some have involved his physical body being forced, coerced, threatened, manipulated, brainwashed and blackmailed into causing differing forms of unpleasantness to others.

In many lifetimes my soul's physical form has been found wandering around many a battlefield, not wanting to be there. However, through the actions of unscrupulous people using their gifts as very persuasive convincers of any ideals they believed in at the time, my soul – as did many other souls who incarnated at various times throughout history when war or any sort of chaos was created – ultimately bore the brunt of their actions. This happened in many a lifetime. I can attest to after having gone back into these lifetimes, some with Yvonne's help and some through my own angelic guidance.

So too this beautiful soul, having been convinced by the hierarchy within his world, had experienced similar scenarios. Likewise, he had been forced, coerced, threatened, manipulated, brainwashed, re-programmed and blackmailed into causing unpleasantness to others, using any means necessary, which undoubtedly included using our families and loved ones to get us to do things we did not want to.

As with my soul Shanti, so too with this reptilian, who had been controlled by overlords and governments. When the overlords said 'Jump,' they said, 'How high?' Both the reptilian soul and my soul have been controlled in many sly, sneaky ways to do the dirty work for our respective controllers.

I spoke of this to our friend, explaining that I understood his ending up here and that all my angelic friends who make up our SR team understood too. And, on behalf of my angelic friends, I was guided to express that we loved him. Yes, we loved him. And all we wished for him was that he would accept this opportunity, which he had prayed for, in his own way, to be set free from this torturous way of life.

This beautiful soul left with ease and was escorted to a realm where he will be able to receive the support and guidance to break free from the life he had become so entangled in, just like Shanti and me. We have had to break through many barriers to get to where we are now, but I would do it all again the same way. By the way, that is in no way a challenge, angels, hehe.

So now our friend had been escorted from the building, it was my turn. Yes, my soul and the reptilian had crossed swords in another lifetime in another world.

My soul had experienced life having been abducted. I have as yet been given no information whether it was in this present or another lifetime but this clearly explains why at times I feel I'm going to float off into the sky, which brings up much fear I can tell you. I have just been shown (23rd June 2022) the scene in Guardians of the Galaxy film where the young boy is beamed up into a spaceship, so this is my confirmation. I was enslaved... I was taken to Mars and put into dungeons deep down inside the planet. There we were experimented on. And other abhorrent things, things that we could never have imagined, happened to us. In truth I would prefer you did not try to imagine. On a personal note, I pray that this sort of experience will very soon come to an end throughout the universe. This is my wish.

The second part of this epic SR was for Shanti and me to forgive the actions of the reptilian who had been directly involved in my soul's experiences on Mars. We did, and it was easy to do so. For whatever has gone on in the past, especially unpleasant experiences, it is in our best interests to forgive those who we perceive do wrong to us.

It's all part of the soul's journey, and as I have said before our soul has to experience both sides of the coin so that in the future our soul then has a choice about how to move forward and evolve.

This is the free will often talked about, which is gifted by God/Goddess or whatever other name you may choose to use for the higher celestial being who created all this.

As I lie on my bed, having said all I was guided to say, while my angelic and galactic friends wrapped up this amazing experience, I sensed that my friends were giving me a message. 'Jeffrey, we now ask you to accept your reward, for you have earned and fully deserve what is about to come into your life.'

Oh, I almost forgot to mention another course served at this SR banquet. I received this via a card reading and a message through a friend on Sunday 4th July. Gina (an alias) first told me that a dark energy had been lifted from my head, and then told me that this person had poisoned my soul's physical body via the use of an apple in another previous lifetime. I felt relieved, because I had been experiencing a mild burning sensation in my mouth over the last few days, which I now know was the physical release of the poison.

Again, forgiveness was required, but it really is becoming easier to forgive.

The person who is mentioned in the above paragraphs was involved in this situation too. Indeed, it has brought about closure and a complete balancing of karma for me and this person.

I think that is everything.

No, hang on, the reptilian has since blessed me with his name. He is called Saul.

Additional Information Regarding the Reptilian Race

Since the coming together of Saul and me I have been told via Yvonne that by doing this SR in the way I did I have opened up an opportunity, a portal for the reptilians to now raise their consciousness, after having been imprisoned for far longer than many of we humans have.

Just look at the reptiles that live on this planet and

see how they have evolved. Very little, if any, evolution has taken place in the last million years or so. This is the same for the reptilian race in the universe, who have been used as tools for their respective leaders in their world. They have been brainwashed so much that they feel nothing. No guilt. But through my connection with Saul, and perhaps through others who are empathetic to their situation, we have been able to destroy this illusion, and now the reptilian masses have the opportunity to leave this world with our help.

They could or can only exist within us when we were or are enveloped in fear, anger or worry, which lowers our vibration and creates an opening for them to enter. As our world evolves the vibration raises within more and more people. So too does the fear retreat, leaving the reptilians nowhere to go and with no option apart from evacuating the human physical bodies they still residing in.

There really is nothing to fear about the possibility of a reptilian residing within your body.

If you are housing a reptilian all this means is that you may well find that everything is a challenge to move forward or to carry out the easiest of tasks in general. This is what the reptilians have been ordered and programmed to do: to cause chaos, doubt and fear within each of us and to suppress our spiritual gifts, so that we remain unaware of what the powers that be in our world are doing. These are many unpleasant and nasty things.

The reptilian can also be compared to the ego, for our ego works on the same principles. When we begin to awaken to our spiritual journey of rediscovery of who we are, the ego will try everything possible to scupper our moving forward by using and reminding us of our greatest fears. Very sneaky is the ego. So too are the reptilians, but in a slightly different way.

Thankfully here on earth, over the last seventy years especially, the awakened population has grown to where it is now. The scales of balance and justice are now swinging in our favour, the favour of the masses: the favour of truth, justice and fairness.

The longevity of the dark forces who have ruled our world for thousands of years is now coming to an end, even to the point that by the time this book is published this may already have happened. It is that close to the end for this part of our collective soul journey.

Every soul on this planet at this time signed up to be here and to experience these times and help raise the vibration of earth. In turn we are then able to help these innocent reptilians move forward on their journey and to break free of this illusion and hopefully reconnect with their families, from who they have been separated from for too long.

Just as many reptilians as we humans have experienced and are experiencing very similar situations. But, as I have stated, as we humans awaken more and more we are able to help our reptilian friends raise their vibration. So together we can help each other break free of the chains that we – both races, and indeed other races too – have been enslaved by for way too long.

When I first heard of our ascension path here on earth, I thought nothing of the rest of the universe and the many different species of beings who are going through many different experiences on different levels of vibrations and dimensions. As we on earth succeed in raising the vibration here, we also help all those other races who are at a lower level to begin their rise to the higher realms of spiritual awareness.

As I keep saying, we are all one. That means every living being, throughout the universe and beyond. We can only ascend if we ascend as one.

Since my initial connection with Saul we, along with my many and varied SR friends, have done a few SRs for our brothers and sisters of the reptilian race.

One by one Saul acts as their leader and guides them to a new world, a new way of living. And I am truly honoured to have played a part in this magical experience.

The SRs have all been unique and so amazing. This very morning, the 9th August, I was made aware of a reptilian who had made herself known to me. This involved my soul, so it was as much a SR to benefit my soul and our journey as it was for this beautiful reptilian soul.

The outstanding factor within every SR that I have done so far was that each reptilian was very confused and was in such a vulnerable place. I do believe that this is what creates the unbalanced state within us when these reptilian friends are present.

> I believe the reptilians are in some way connected, to our experiences of dementia and related issues. I will add more information as and when I get it.

When we are in a state of fear and worry we subconsciously open ourselves to be a home for a reptilian.

When we are calm, at peace and flowing with a vibration of love we are in our true state and the reptilian will have to leave our body. This is becoming easier to understand for me, and hopefully it will be for you too, as you come to know these beings, for they too have beautiful souls. They have simply been subdued and suppressed, as we humans have, and possibly other races throughout the universe.

I have seen this in action and seen the proof. One SR I recently did involved a person who did not know that they were housing a reptilian. The other person in the relationship told me that their partner's behaviour had changed in such negative ways. They did not want to go out and they felt very unstable, angry, fearful and vulnerable, to the point of paranoia.

When I had a chat with this person the conversation was the conduit to keep me there for a few minutes so the reptilian could connect with me. Exactly like trapped souls do, they find a way to get to the person who can help them move on by using them as a taxi when they know their time is running out. This was the case with this conversation.

I was made aware of this connection a few days later and completed a very swift SR, again with much help from Saul.

When chatting to the partner of the person who released this reptilian a few weeks later, they said that they had noticed a change of behaviour in a positive way, as if a big weight had been lifted from their shoulders – which in truth it had, in the form of a reptilian.

It's the 5th of February 2022.

It's the sixth anniversary of Dad's passing. As I sit at my laptop in readiness to add this latest piece, I feel in a much better place after the most amazing healing session, which in part brought this information to my attention yesterday, the 4th February.

I have been under the weather for two weeks, which has lowered my vibration so much so that unbeknownst to me another reptilian brother had been forced to step into my physical body and had created another unique set of issues for me to deal with. These have caused me the maximum level of upheaval and have dragged me back into the third dimension without my even being aware that I had been. This has occurred because the releasing I have done has been very unpleasant and has caused me to dip into a place of fear.

This is all the reptilian controllers have needed, and it has given them the go signal. Once my vibration had lowered sufficiently it seemed as if I was back to square one. This is slightly untrue, but it did offer up some alternative experiences that I had to overcome to break free of the reptilian's firm grasp.

The main point is that while we may reach a vibrational level at which the reptilian has nowhere to go, so it has to exit our body, it is for us to focus on keeping our vibration at a level where the reptilian controllers are unable to infiltrate our bodies with another reptilian until we master the higher vibrations and stay there. This is our ongoing challenge.

This is the priceless information that I have been blessed with. This has been a very challenging experience indeed, and it has again shown me how sneaky those who are controlling the reptilians can be.

This was an experience in which I had to use all my spiritual tools and know-how. And even then I needed help from Yvonne via a dream experience to see this issue through to completion, after gaining the strength to break free from it.

My Brother Jack's SR ~ from 1964 to 31st July 2021

I WAKE FEELING very emotional after having had a very deep healing session with Yvonne on Wednesday, with lots to embrace and accept, along with a vast amount of information, which has overwhelmed me slightly. It's understandable, with my recent move and so much more going on.

Now I am awake I begin to feel and receive energies and messages, all pertaining to my brother Jack. He passed after only twenty-four hours of life and just months before I came along. I have done so much work to help Mum and Dad complete their healing process, but have never thought about Jack much until now.

Yesterday (Friday) I started to get information reminding me about Dad and his rivalry with his brother and my uncle Ian. It was as if Dad was in competition with Uncle Ian for his dad's love and attention. My uncle didn't do anything out of the ordinary to gain his dad's love, but my dad did all sorts of things to get his dad's attention.

My uncle Ian was a very laid-back person, but my dad was the opposite. Obviously this was due to the experiences of their souls in this and other lifetimes.

As I now sit and write I realise that this was Dad's issue to resolve, and it had nothing to do with Uncle Ian. Dad, as I now know, was a very insecure and sensitive person and felt the need to get his dad's attention for some reason. When I investigated the core of this issue I could see that it went back into a lack of self-worth, among other factors, as it did with me when I investigated my need to gain Dad's love in my way.

Dad was jealous because he believed Uncle Ian to be his dad's favourite and felt the need to gain his dad's attention by doing things he didn't necessarily want to, just as I have done with my dad. An ancestral issue to be healed here, I think.

As Dad was jealous of his brother Ian, so I was jealous of my brother Jack.

This is very uncomfortable to write, but it's the truth. I was competing with someone who wasn't even alive, such was the depth of my insecurity. This issue with my brother Jack goes back into other lifetimes, which I will not bore you with. This issue was in dire need of attention, and today I gave it just that.

I woke up feeling very unbalanced and emotional. I felt Jack around me and then the penny dropped. We had done so much healing work for Mum and Dad but had done almost nothing to heal the connection between Jack and me...

I'm being reminded that everything is in divine and perfect order.

I then sensed that firstly part of Jack's soul had become

trapped through fear when his physical body passed on and secondly through Mum and Dad not wanting to let go of their firstborn. This is understandable, but an unhealthy attachment was formed.

I now realise that this part of Jack's soul had been with us since his passing. When Mum and Dad also passed the attachment between them was still evident, but it was left to me to help this part of Jack's soul move on.

From that moment we started to do our healing. Alas, I knew nothing about this until today.

Being jealous of someone is an uncomfortable issue to deal with and to accept. It brings up all those dark emotions and feelings that need to be embraced so we can then let them go, which sets us free in the process.

It was an emotional SR this morning. I began the SR by inviting my angelic friends in, to prepare the room for the departure of Jack's soul and to create the perfect scene, so he would feel as calm as possible. I was blessed with the vision of Mum and Dad coming for and holding Jack in their arms, which was a very touching and emotional moment.

This SR concluded within minutes, but the main thing was for me to realise that I had no need to compete with my brother – or anyone else, for that matter. Throughout our soul's journey we have had many incarnations and experienced many differing situations – some nice, some not so nice. The awareness I have been blessed with has not only brought a long-standing issue with my brother's soul to an end but also for my ancestors, through Dad's family line. Only God knows how far back through this line this issue goes.

My guided and intuitive actions today have now brought closure for many. I am so grateful and honoured to be of service in this way, and to have played my part.

It was not the most exciting SR I've done, but the blessings around it have been monumental for my ancestors and me.

The Gas Chamber SR ~ from *circa* 1979 to 19th August 2021

I HAVE VISITED Cleveleys near Blackpool frequently over the last two weeks, and these visits have brought up so much emotional stuff for me to release.

However, on Thursday 19th August I started to see the reasoning behind my frequent visits and how magical this process has again been. On this visit I had a paddle in the sea, which released all the negativity that no longer served me, including a large dose of abandonment issues.

Having released that lot, I was ready for some food. The regular cafe I normally frequent was full, so I ventured further down the main street, crossed the tramlines and came upon a lovely little cafe.

While in the cafe a little dog kept coming over wanting to be stroked, which I happily obliged.

There was a definite connection with this angel. But I didn't understand what that was until yesterday evening, when I was called upon to do a SR for part of my soul that, unbeknownst to me, had connected to me at the cafe.

This is where it gets magical, because the *taxi* for this

part of my soul was in fact the dog, who is called Toffee.

As I chatted with the lady who was Toffee's guardian I found out that Toffee had been brought over from Poland via her friend, who looks after stray dogs there.

Toffee had obviously been treated unpleasantly, but now he was in the care of this lady and was now being looked after as he deserved.

Now this is where it gets interesting as I go back a long way into my childhood.

As a family we would come to Cleveleys for our summer holidays, and we did this for around eight years. These were the happiest memories I have of my childhood, because what with everything that was going on within our family and all the negative experiences we had very few periods of joy.

I state categorically, though, while my life and my family's life have been tough, it was exactly what our combined souls needed to experience to further our souls' journey. So the releasing I have been doing for over twenty years has been for me, obviously, but has also been for my parents and my ancestors. I feel very honoured to have played my part in this way.

At the age of fourteen I had to go to the dentist for some teeth out under gas. I had had an unpleasant experience with gas while having some teeth removed when I was around eight years old, and it was also bad this time around. The upshot was that I did not like the gas and I fought it until it overcame me. Each time I experienced the gas it was preparing me for this moment here and now, to understand this part of my soul's journey and its experiences, so that as I write I can physically release any memories from that time long gone.

As I was walking with Mum and Dad along the promenade at Cleveleys, just after my visit to the dentist, I began to smell gas. I asked Mum if she could smell it, but her reaction wasn't what I had hoped. Basically, Mum thought I was going daft. This was understandable, I suppose, but the way she reacted did affect me. I felt very angry that Mum didn't believe me. This is one issue I have had to deal with during these visits to Cleveleys to make way for the amazing closure you are about to read about.

This issue came up during a healing with Yvonne, where she told me that Mum's reaction to my question had brought up deep emotions within her regarding a past life – the same past life I was being reminded of each time I smelt the gas.

The lifetime was during WWII, and it involved the concentration camp Auschwitz II-Birkenau in occupied Poland. This is also where the abandonment issue peaks.

My initial statement on the promenade brought up emotions for Mum, and no doubt Dad too. For in that life they, as in this life, were my parents and I was the child. Mum and Dad put me on a train, believing I was going to be saved from the gas chambers, but their plan sadly failed. My physical body was, as many others were, put to death in the chambers.

No wonder I didn't like the gas used by the dentists each time they removed my teeth.

So how did my soul come to be connected to Toffee? And why was Toffee brought to Cleveleys, of all places, where the initial connection to this lifetime appeared?

Firstly, there are no coincidences. This is another example of the creative powers of God/Goddess or whatever you call the celestial being who created this world and others. I have said many times that we are all connected, but for this earth experience our soul chooses we appear to become separate. This is just an illusion, but it's necessary. We are blessed with connections to other souls, who we incarnate with often, to help each other's souls with their lessons.

So my physical body passed in the gas chambers, and it is very frightening to know that part of my soul became trapped in that illusion. After this period of history ended anyone visiting this camp, or any of the other camps, can easily be attached to by any trapped soul while walking through the empty chambers and the ruins of the camp if it in is their soul contract to do so.

Now Toffee may well have been found in the vicinity of the camp connecting to my soul directly. But it is also possible, as the title of this book states, that there may well have been a few physical bodies that my soul attached to before finally getting to the cafe in Cleveleys.

The fact that Toffee brought this part of my soul from Poland really amazes me, and there is a definite connection between us.

It is a timely piece of information for me that not only can humans be a taxi for trapped souls but indeed, as I have come to experience, a crystal can be and now a dog can be too. I'm now being shown that anything that has a soul, be it a tree, a flower or whatever, it can also be a beacon of light for the souls to connect with, as part of their journey to the person who can help them move on.

The Crystal Magic SR ~ 15th August 2021

I WILL ADD this little piece because again it shows the subtle ways in which things can slightly differ on a spiritual journey. Each one so amazing.

I went to a crystal shop in Leyland one day last week and found myself being drawn to two crystal towers, one small and one large. When holding them I felt they were a pair, a female form and a male form. They were coming home with me, they made that quite clear. The amazing thing about this was that Jaime had bought them at two different locations.

Thankfully Jaime followed her guidance to buy both crystals for her shop. Then I was guided to visit the shop and to take them with me on the next part of our journey, for crystals are also on a journey. When our soul contract ends these crystals will move on, perhaps to someone else or somewhere else.

Yes, I do believe that crystals have a soul. Again, this is how we connect with souls from our soul group. The souls of these crystals obviously sensed a connection with me and used Jaime as a taxi to get them to her shop.

The Pain Release SR ~ from 2011 to 9th September 2021

HAVING WOKEN UP around 6 30 a.m. this morning 9th September 2021, I knew what I needed to do and where I was to go, but a part of me was resisting. As always when I get this feeling, I know it's exactly what I need to do. Today was no different. So with the resistance or the ego trying its best to stop me, I headed off to the seaside once again, with no real idea why or what for, but knowing that it would make itself known to me very quickly indeed.

I started to receive thoughts and visions of a past life with Dad, who in that life was a very strict schoolteacher in Russia in the 1800s. My dad in this life was my dad in this lifetime that I am writing about now. I was the child in both lifetimes. Now, in this lifetime, which I now believe to have been the beginning of this specific cycle, Dad taught me, but taught with a rod of iron. Anything I got wrong I was punished for. He hit me many times during my childhood and my teenage years as I grew up.

This specific lifetime was brought up by Yvonne during a healing over ten years ago. During my latest healing session, on 7th September 2021, we talked about this lifetime once again. Only this time just days later the very timid soul from that lifetime actually made himself known to me.

Unbeknownst to me, this part of my soul connected to me during the healing session with Yvonne. So this beautiful soul has been hiding away for over ten years, waiting patiently for the perfect time to appear, but all the while affecting me greatly through the emotions and mental abuse he had suffered in that lifetime and other lifetimes where this cycle continued to play out. These were emotions and mental issues that I had no idea I was carrying and releasing.

We really have no idea how much baggage we are carrying on behalf of our soul and how much healing and releasing is needed. I dare say that if we did, we would run off in the other direction very quickly indeed. I would, that's for sure.

Everyone will have different amounts of healing to do, due to the unique journey of our souls, so most of us won't have as much as I have had to do, I hope.

The outcome for my soul in that lifetime was that he didn't live long into adulthood, and from the constant beatings he became frightened of life itself. This was pretty much like how I felt as a child in this present lifetime. He eventually committed suicide. This has only just come to me as I type this sentence. Many emotions are surfacing too.

It's amazing how our soul maps their journey out in such detail. The experiences in the life that instigated this SR have in some ways been replicated in this lifetime and experienced by my physical body. I have said before that as a child I was preparing myself for the arrival of Shanti through my experiences. When we merged in September 1999 I became the vessel to help Shanti heal and release all his excess baggage from his universal travels, and Shanti was here to help me heal and release all my ancestral issues. We were ready to begin our journey together without delay.

Mum used to tell me that as a child of two years of age I spat at Dad and that he hit me. As a child of nine Dad again hit me with his belt. I have no idea why.

I have had to work through forgiveness regarding these two incidents each time they have come to the surface. I have come to understand why Dad did these things and have accepted them. These actions are actions that should never happen, but sadly they do.

Yvonne told me that my soul as the two-year-old was uncomfortable in his physical body and showed his distress. Dad reacted, and I know he regretted his actions as soon as he hit me.

As the nine-year-old, Mum and Dad left me alone for the first time while they went out with friends. As I have said earlier, I was at the stage in my life where I was frightened of everything, including being left alone in the house. So I asked Julie, who lived next door, if I could stay with her until they came home, she said 'Yes.'

I thought nothing more about it, but when Mum and Dad came home early Dad was enraged. They had obviously rung our house to see if I was all right. To get no answer must have caused them to fear the worst, but

I had no idea of this. After all, I was just a child.

Only very recently have I come to understand why Dad reacted as he did.

It all stems back to the loss of Jack after only twenty-four hours of life.

I wouldn't know where to even begin to try and understand how they felt after this horrific experience. Every time I went out, even as an adult, they must have been worrying incessantly until I came home, either as an adult from work or from the pub, or as a child from being out playing or at school.

If I arrived home later that the stated time their fear and worry must have ramped up dramatically, and understandably so. They were in their way trying to make sure that nothing happened to me. The last thing they wanted was for something to happen that would cause them to lose another child.

I now fully understand why Dad hit me. However, through those two incidents Dad created karma for himself. As I mentioned in the previous SR, when a negative action is taken the perpetrator will accrue karma.

So he didn't get away with his actions scot-free. But, as I have said earlier, after each moment when the red mist descended he instantly felt guilty and regretted his actions. These feelings will have caused Dad much heartache and will have also caused illness to manifest in his physical body later in life.

In the Russian lifetime Dad again accrued much karma for his actions each time he beat me for getting the answer wrong, or whatever it was that didn't match his expectations of me.

I will now return to today and to my short trip to the seaside. As I have said, the information about this pain came to me. The trapped part of my soul made his presence felt just as we were coming into a slight traffic jam on the motorway. This gave me ample time during the rest of our journey to explain and to talk to this part of my soul. I asked him to forgive, to reassure and to express to him that this illusion would now come to a very swift end when we arrived at our destination, Cleveleys.

Once I had stepped onto the beach and called all my SR friends to help and bless us with their gifts, the SR was over in literally seconds. Dad had come to escort my soul home, which was beautiful. For this cycle to be ended at Cleveleys was poetic. And even more so to release all the pain from those lifetimes where this issue was continuously being played out, over who knows how many lifetimes.

Cleveleys is a place in this lifetime where we as a family had the happiest of times. It was also perfect timing for me and my soul's journey, for I only realised while on the journey to the seaside that this pain was my comfort blanket, which I was holding on to.

Yes, it was my comfort blanket. I didn't want to let it go because it felt like the last tenuous link to Dad in this lifetime. Crazy, eh?

Yet it is so understandable, for when we experience something, anything, even the darkest, most unpleasant experiences, we become used to it. But when something much nicer begins to materialise, we begin to fear it.

There are two reasons these feelings can arise:
1. Breaking out of any cycle, especially one where abuse of any type has occurred, can be challenging. When it has occurred over many lifetimes it becomes more challenging with each lifetime that passes, while any specific cycle is still playing out.
2. And feelings can arise from any fear that has been created by experiences in lifetimes of abuse. While real, these experiences may have already stopped occurring in the present lifetime, but the fear and other negative emotions must be allowed to come to the surface to be acknowledged and then released. Until this release has been completed and the victim has attained a level of spiritual awareness about why these feelings had arisen in this present lifetime they will undoubtedly still feel safer experiencing the horrific experiences of their previous lifetimes.

This is what reiki and other various forms of natural healing can help us to achieve when we are ready. They help us clear emotionally, mentally and physically, and this helps us reconnect to the spiritual being that we are, always have been and will always be.

The result: we can enjoy a better life more and more as we release the emotional and mental baggage, one layer at a time, that is our reward as we do the work necessary.

This is exactly what I have experienced throughout this lifetime as both man and boy. Even as an adult I was fearful of Dad because of his actions towards me as a child.

When Dad had his stroke in 2008 I became his main carer, but even during this period I could not rest easily for fear of him doing something unpleasant to me, which eventually manifested into my reality. This is exactly what I mean by talking about fearing something that has already run its course. When we continue to focus on those fears, we can manifest them.

While I was acting as Dad's main carer he attempted suicide a few times and threatened it on other occasions, all to keep his control over me. This issue is entwined within the lifetime in Russia.

In that lifetime Dad lost his wife and I lost a mum, just as we have in this present life. Dad did his best but his anger, his frustration or whatever negative thoughts that filled his head were always directed at me, just as has happened in this present life. I was directly in the firing line. They say that we hurt the ones closest to us. This is so very true in my experience.

It is for the victim or the soul who is on the receiving end of the abuse to bring these cycles to an end, but in a way that no karma is created. We need to stand up for ourselves by subtly taking our power back one step at a time.

One day Dad came at me in an angry state. 'What do I do?' I said to myself. Instinctively I reached out and managed to get hold of his wrists. As gently as I could, I pushed him onto the bed and said, 'I'm not here for you to use as a punchbag.'

Dad was shocked at my actions, but alas his increased state of dementia quickly helped him forget what had happened. In a way I'm glad he did forget because it was so uncomfortable for me to contemplate.

This whole experience occurred in just a few seconds. Had I more time to decide how to react I would have probably allowed him to hit me. He had done it before, but to be fair it didn't hurt. However, standing up for myself as I did helped me take some of my power back and instigate the beginning of the end to this cycle, although it took a few more years to achieve.

So the accumulated pain (and the emotional and mental baggage) I carried for over ten years associated with this specific issue has been well and truly left on the beach at Cleveleys. Not only will I benefit from my actions, but Dad will too. So will Mum. Knowing this makes me feel so humbled that I have been able to bring this cycle and many other cycles to an end for my soul family and my ancestors.

> All happening at the perfect time, in the perfect way, in the perfect place.

A new beginning – a new era – has appeared for me today, and I will grasp this opportunity with both hands.

Thank you, Dad, for everything we have experienced throughout our soul's journey together. You truly have been one of my greatest teachers. I love you so much.

The Multi-pickup SR ~ 13th September 2021

THIS, I BELIEVE, has happened to me before. However, this is the first time I have been aware of it, pickup by pickup, as it unfolded.

I started my day visiting the crystal shop I have frequented over the last few months. I had a lovely chat with Jaime and Nic. I didn't realise I had picked up a fare until I arrived at Debbie's. She had company – another friend, who we both know. The conversation with our friend was short, but enough time passed for what I believe to be a trapped soul to connect with me from her via Debbie.

Then Debbie, for some reason, sat on the couch facing me – not her normal seat – but again it was necessary for her to transfer the soul to me during our chat. This took a bit longer for the soul to trust me, but eventually he did.

On the way back I stopped off at the shop for some provisions then headed home.

Once I was home I began to prepare for a SR. This was one for a few souls who had all connected with me at various times throughout the day via different taxi drivers. They were the soul from the crystal shop and the three connected to Debbie and our friend. One was a reptilian brother, who I was particularly honoured to help, as I am with all souls. The SR was swift, and again I used the physical sword of truth that was gifted to me by my Knights Templar friends. A swift and magical conclusion was attained.

Now I know this may not be earth-shattering information, but realising that this is how the souls are now beginning to find their way to me by any means possible, and in larger numbers, is an eye-opener for me. I know the total number of souls only came to four, but they came to me via four different routes all in one day. This I take as a sign that things are going to ramp up regarding SR work done freely, without financial payment as an exchange. My light is obviously shining brighter so that more souls can find their way to me in the future and for me to be guided to visit places to connect with souls as well. Fabulous.

Hours later...

Now, after having completed the SR I have just written about, I began to feel very cold around my left knee and all the way down my right side. I didn't really take much notice, to be honest. However when it is SR time, time waits for no man.

I woke around 6 a.m. and was soon made aware that the two areas of coldness were a young child around my knee and the man down my right side, both had been involved in an unpleasant experience.

On one of my walks in nature I had connected to the child's trapped soul. This connection happened a few years ago.

The child's trapped soul has been with me since then, waiting patiently in the shadows, until the time was right so the coming together of these two souls could be helped to understand and at least begin to forgive themselves and the other soul involved, otherwise the SR would not be completed.

Again, as with every SR I have done thus far, forgiveness was the main issue to be ironed out. I spoke at length with these two souls. The child was so frightened when I spoke to her, but I did reassure her that nothing nor anyone from that lifetime could hurt her anymore.

It does take courage for the souls who have been the victim in unpleasant experiences to trust me and my angelic friends. But I am so glad that they do eventually trust my words and the presence of so many pure, loving angels, and that one (or more) of their loved ones in spirit form also come to escort the souls home.

The SR was again completed swiftly after I had explained to the souls and reassured them that it was safe to move on. I was going to say that the child was more important. However both the child and the gentleman had very different issues to deal with during our chat. Briefly, the child obviously had a fear of something like this happening again. The gentleman had to deal with regret, so both had to be treated with compassion.

At this point I will remind you that we are all connected. Whatever the gentleman had caused he felt it as much as the child, but in different ways, obviously.

When every human realises and accepts this statement below as truth, then and only then will all these unpleasant experiences stop, in this world as in other worlds where this statement isn't fully understood:

The energies that are emitted from what our soul causes to happen to others through words, thoughts or actions, especially if they are unpleasant or horrific, flow outwardly as a ripple in the water. These energies are not only felt here on earth but throughout the universe and beyond. The same happens when something positive happens or is said. It ripples out through this world, the universe and beyond. Only when we forgive rather than seek revenge will this world heal.

When you have finally understood this statement, how do you then choose to move forward on your unique path?

On a personal note, I pray that this time comes very soon.

The Suicide Cycle SR ~ Date Unknown to 15th September 2021

THIS ONGOING ISSUE regarding one of my soul's current and toughest cycles to break is that of suicide. As I type, the origin of this issue has yet to come to my attention, but it goes back at least a few thousand years.

While flipping through the TV channels last night a programme piqued my curiosity. I didn't watch the programme but felt something was now being brought to the surface for me to address. While reading the short synopsis of the programme I felt energies around me. When I asked my guides if this programme and the person involved had something to do with these energies, I got a very clear 'Yes.' So I continued to ask questions to help me understand what needed doing, when and where.

The *when* was minutes later as I prepared my room after calling in my SR friends, lying down and then starting the process of SR. I will add that my soul, while I had been sleeping earlier in the day, had gone to the place where this gentleman had passed by committing suicide. He had brought back the trapped part of the gentleman's soul, which just happened to be part of my soul too.

Now it is my belief that when a soul passes after having committed suicide the part of the soul that doesn't become trapped, immediately comes back to earth and enters another physical body to continue its journey to help it awaken sufficiently. This is so that it and the physical body can realise that this is not the way. It has taken my soul many incarnations to get to this point, where I am aware that this cycle is in dire need of breaking, and so it will be this time.

I spoke to the trapped soul the same way as I do with any soul who is seeking to be set free from the illusion they are trapped in, regardless of the actions that have caused them to be in this position. Like I say, it didn't take long to find out that he had committed suicide and to feel the emotions surrounding this drastic option.

Feeling worthless, powerless, unsupported, and living with a feeling of utter despair, had led this gentleman to follow through with this idea. When finding out that this was part of my soul, the cycle of suicide surfaced and confirmed my thoughts about how this person died, for he is quite well known. But the truth around this (and many other events throughout history) has been conveniently hidden.

Now I have written about a few of my soul's lifetimes where suicide was the outcome, and as time goes by I am being made aware there were many, many more lifetimes where this fate has befallen my soul. They are all a part of my soul's journey.

There are so many nuances involved with this issue of

suicide and so many scenarios that can bring any person to the point of attempting to do this to themselves, let alone succeeding in doing so.

My dad attempted suicide a few times in what was his present life because the woman he loved, my mum Louie, had a very long battle with cancer and other ailments, and he knew he couldn't do anything to save her. All he could do was watch her deteriorate over many years, as I did. He just couldn't cope.

I really can understand why Dad attempted suicide, and rather than feel anger towards him, as I did after his first attempt, I learnt to see that it takes courage to attempt or to go through with suicide. Whichever way you go about it, suicide cannot be a pleasant experience and the soul will almost certainly become trapped.

I will use the life of James IV, who died at Flodden, as an example (which I have written about in Book One). Now I know he died on the field of battle, but I have come to understand that being killed is in some way a lesser form of suicide. Had James survived, he would have most likely have committed suicide. Sometimes on a field of battle some have no desire to be there. This was James's poisoned chalice, and that of many other leaders throughout history as well.

He had to be seen to do the right thing to protect his countrymen and women. This is a similar outcome for the gentleman I'm doing this SR for. He was literally forced into a conflict he had no desire to get involved with, but the constant barrage of abuse aimed at him and his people by the perpetrators finally forced his hand.

His country was being targeted in such a way that

many innocent people were killed. This was the sole reason why he finally reacted.

His actions caused many more to die. This is the core reason for his sense of worthlessness. He felt that he was in a no-win situation and chose the lesser of the two evils. Had he allowed the barrage of attacks to continue, his country would have been wiped out. But, whatever he chose, it would have cost many lives.

At this part of my soul's journey, it wasn't as aware spiritually as I am now. Hypothetically, had this scenario surfaced in the here and now, my decision would have been easy. Due to the law of karma, I would have stepped down as leader and allowed someone else to take the leadership role. There is no way that I would consciously create more negative karma for myself.

My soul's actions in this no-win situation created a lot of karma, which has had to be worked through to balance it. I do feel therefore that the trapped soul of the gentleman has been brought back now, simply because the time is right for me to bring this cycle to an end in this lifetime, which balances the karma too.

The end of the cycle: no more committing suicide.

Let me tell you there have been times throughout my present life where I have thought long and hard about committing suicide, but thankfully something has always happened to stop me going too far. Personally, I don't think I would have been able to go through with it, but you never know what can happen. For example, I have had a lifetime where I used suicide as a weapon to control a lady who I was in love with. She didn't feel the same way, so I threatened to hang myself. I didn't mean to, but I ended up going through the motions because the lady thought I was joking. But due to circumstances beyond my control something happened, and I ended up hanging myself, not my preferred outcome. So anything can happen when you are in such a desperate situation.

Back to the current SR.

The whole SR took just minutes to complete, but the groundwork that was necessary took longer. The soul went swiftly and now I await this part of my soul's return, cleansed and cleared of all the emotions from the lifetime I am writing of. As more particles of my soul return, the closer my soul comes to being whole and the closer to ascending from this realm. This is our goal.

As I write, I am releasing through my physical body the emotions that my soul endured in that lifetime. I hope that this challenging cycle is bringing an end to this part of my soul's journey, so I can enjoy and move forward in life without those unpleasant feelings surfacing at a moment's notice.

The blessing when we do this inner work is to heal and to release our soul's emotional baggage, for this is what the physical body was in part created for.

Soul Retrieval Work ~ Moving to a New Level

OVER THE LAST few weeks, in between doing lots of inner work on myself, I find myself doing more SR work than before. It's an obvious step as I gain in confidence and as my vibration rises. I am also blessed with more connections to angels from higher dimensions coming to guide and work through me, all of which further boosts my confidence and increases my excitement about the future SR work that we as a team do.

This began in the last few weeks, when I have done SR work not for the odd one or two but for many, almost on a daily basis.

My reptilian friend and guide Saul, my soul and other angels are now bringing in souls who have become trapped in places I would find very difficult to access physically. Doing this via my angelic friends, who have now become the taxi for many souls seeking my guidance, is such a perfect option. And more souls are being attracted to my light and my vibration as I go about my daily experiences. As well as the times where I have work to do for myself while also doing my inner work, souls coming through for help on top of everything can sometimes be a little too much.

Also during the last few weeks, I have bought more crystals, three orgone pyramids, a picture of Buddha and various other items. These all enhance the energies in my home so that we do each SR justice with great care, which they all fully deserve.

Now I wish to share some information about our reptilian friends because more and more of them, especially since I have had help from Saul, are now finding themselves lost and in need of help. With the vibration of this world rising, with more people raising their vibration and healing, with them shedding layers of their soul and dealing with ancestral issues, it is becoming more uncomfortable for our reptilian friends to remain within their physical bodies.

Let me stress categorically that these foreign bodies have been forced upon us by dark forces. These are perhaps the elites of the reptilian race or indeed of another race altogether. But whoever they are their energies are at a much higher level, and they are able to force, brainwash and blackmail their lesser brothers and sisters to take part in this massive undertaking against their will.

A reptilian can enter our body when fear reaches a level that resonates with its own vibration, which is a very low, dense energy. The reptilian is then attracted to the person or animal and slips in uninvited.

When installed in a physical body the reptilian will have been programmed to disrupt the vessel it resides in, to halt its progress in awakening and raising its own consciousness. In some ways this is likened to the ego.

As the ego serves to control us through fear and doubt, by the same token this is the agenda that has been programmed into the reptilian.

Now I have come to understand that people in powerful positions around the world for many hundreds or thousands of years have had a particular type of reptilian merge with them, obviously to create havoc for that person but to also create and wreak havoc on those people they have control over. This is how the dark forces have controlled the masses.

However, the world is now changing. The energies are raising, so our reptilian friends are now being forced from our human bodies as more of us awaken and raise our vibration above the level of fear. Hence the reason why my SR work has stepped up a level.

As more people raise their vibration to a level that forces the reptilians to leave their bodies, the reptilians are left adrift ... until thankfully Saul and other awakened reptilians can seek them out and connect them with me or anyone else who has been blessed with the gifts to do this work so I can play my part in helping to set them free from their very long and unpleasant ordeal.

I have stated in an earlier piece that our reptilian brothers and sisters have been controlled at a deeper level that even we humans have, and that is saying something. As the information comes out about the reptilians and what they are supposed to have done, some may see these angels as the bad guys. My belief is they have been used and controlled and are now being set up as the scapegoats by their oppressors, again just as we have been by governments.

I urge you, as in all situations, to please use your

intuition in all matters rather than listening to and taking on board someone else's beliefs.

Including mine.

Every reptilian brother and sister I have had the true honour of helping via SR is so beautiful, so vulnerable and so in need of our help so that they can fully remember who they are.

They are made from the same energy as we are.

We are all connected. We are all part of the oneness. Even those who have forced the reptilians and we humans into doing things we have had no desire to do are made from the same energy as we are.

The Cellar SR ~ 13th October 2021

THIS SR, AS with all the other ones I have done, has gifted me such magical insights with respect to how powerful a specific SR was, especially the SR I did at Boleskine House in Scotland, which I wrote about in Book One.

First, I will share with you my experiences within the cellar and then expand on the similarities regarding the Boleskine SR.

The venue for this SR was Le Chic beauty salon in Chorley. I spoke to the part-owner Lisa yesterday and got some information about the goings-on within the cellar.

On arrival I had already been notified by my Arcturian friends that they would be of help today, and it was to prove that they were very helpful indeed.

I have come to understand that one of my Arcturian friend's gifts is that of being able to help with truly deep and dark energies, entities and the removal thereof, which was right up their street today.

I liken them to bleach. They get right to the core and

cleanse thoroughly and very quickly with no messing (this is just my quirky way of expressing their divine gifts).

I had a brief chat with Lisa before going down into the cellar. Lisa is just opening up to her spiritual path but does receive and see visions, which proved invaluable during this SR. The cellar was like a building site, perhaps because there was lots of building work going on down there hehe. I began by entering each room (there were six in total) to see what I could pick up energetically.

In the first room there was an annexe-type room that was maybe four feet wide and maybe ten feet long. It was something like a hidden passage with a doorway. That's how best to describe it.

This is where I connected to a young boy who was very scared indeed. I gently asked him to come out of there and come with me and that nothing could hurt him any longer. The SR for this soul was done surprisingly quickly after he understood how his soul had become trapped. He was obviously ready to go once I had connected with him.

The other rooms didn't feel too bad energetically, but in one of them I began to put reiki symbols into the walls, floor and ceiling. These are very powerful symbols, which I have only used very sparingly in my SR work thus far. I then backtracked to the room where the young boy was and proceeded to place the symbols in this room too.

The room where a fireplace was situated started to make me realise how powerful this cellar's energies were, and not in a good way. As I faced the fireplace I sensed that this had been used for rituals and human sacrifice.

On receiving this information Archangel Michael made his presence felt and invited me to allow him to step into me as an instrument for him to close this portal. He offered my physical body protection while doing this.

When this information came through I then started to use my preprepared concoction of essential oils and spring water, which I had asked my angels to enhance in their own unique ways. I started to say the Lord's Prayer and placed more symbols into the fireplace and into the area where the table once stood. I sprayed more of the elixir I had made earlier then my Arcturian friends appeared. All this was in conjunction with many SR teammates from all realms, including the beautiful Seraphim, Jesus and Quan Yin. We had such a very powerful team, which we needed to help remove and clear this seemingly dormant cellar.

However, I now know that the cellar had been a place for dark ritual worship. And during their rituals the people or beings performing them had also opened a portal for unpleasant entities to come through, whether they had meant to or not.

I must add that when I completed my first visit, which included placing the symbols in, after having helped the souls who had connected with me to move on, it was necessary to give my angelic friends time to further enhance the cellar with their formidable light to coax out those souls who were in hiding.

As I set off to go down into the cellar a second time I invited Lisa and Emma, her business partner, to come with me, to see if they felt anything.

Lisa said she heard someone screaming. I understood later that this was part of her soul, which had become trapped in another lifetime. So this is why she came back to this building, to bring closure to this lifetime. There was also a message that came through Lisa from the mother of the young boy who connected with me at first, thanking us for setting him free. Very humbling to hear.

As I stepped through the doorway of the next room, Lisa felt an unpleasant energy and didn't want to enter. As she said this, I was facing the corner of the room, and in sync we both said, 'The tall man.'

Now Lisa had mentioned during one of our chats that there was a tall man who was present at times while she was working, which made her feel uncomfortable. This was the same man now making himself known to both Lisa and me. I sensed him standing in the corner, but Lisa saw him. Lisa said, 'He is asking for help to set him free.'

I asked Lisa and Emma to go back upstairs while I helped with the man's request. We both felt he was the leader of this cult gathering. There were feelings from Lisa that he had been hanged. I expanded on this because I felt that he had been made to do this himself after having been interrupted during one of the ritual gatherings by a lynch mob and was immediately forced to put a rope around his own neck.

He was very reticent, which surprised me, because having been the perpetrator of many horrific acts I would have expected to feel more aggressive energies from him. However, more information gifted to me revealed that on my initial visit into the cellar, and in conjunction with my SR teammates, we had initiated a dissolving of the illusion that he and the other souls were trapped in. Basically, they started to see through the illusion and see the reality they were in and accordingly asked for help.

This was another priceless piece of information. Thank you, angels. Thankfully he too went swiftly to the light, which brought the SR to a wonderful conclusion.

Now here are the similarities I have been shown between this SR and the Boleskine SR involving Aleister Crowley.

Before I visited Scotland and the ex-home of Mr Crowley there had in recent years been two fires within a short space of time, which had left the house in ruins and open to the elements. This, I believe, took some of the sting out of the energies I would face when I went there.

The areas in the house where the unpleasantness occurred were open to the elements, so the wind, rain, snow and sun would have started to clear some of the energies. The same goes for the stable at the back where the portal, which was opened over a hundred years before, was situated. However, the portal, until my SR teammates closed it, would have constantly churned out unpleasant entities.

During my visit to Boleskine House I used many crystals and a lot of holy water. I was guided to say the Lord's Prayer, which I did many times. And I used a full bag of sage and placed many reiki symbols in the buildings and had the help of my many SR teammates. Such a powerful combination of tools to clear the area.

Having had today's experiences in the cellar, I know I was in no way ready to step into the building where the portal was at Boleskine, but I was ready to step into the room where the portal was in the cellar.

This alone shows me how far I have advanced regarding doing SR work, for which I feel so grateful and truly blessed.

The two SRs, the one at Boleskine and the SR in the cellar, are similar. But, having gained more knowledge and understanding of SR work, I realise how powerful the Boleskine SR would have been had the building not suffered from fire damage and had not been open to the elements. It would have taken a truly powerful team to clear it. Thankfully the fires and the elements had taken the sting out of this SR.

Boleskine was all in the open and above ground.

The cellar, which was smaller in area, was like a sealed room below ground.

There was nowhere for the energies to go, so the energies built up and built up until Lisa had had enough and sought to call upon someone to help her deal with the issue. This all happened at the perfect time, for had it not been dealt with the energies would have started to seep out from the cellar and the salon, which would have had a truly negative effect on the houses and the area around the cellar.

Again, this was so very powerful in its own right. Thankfully it is all hypothetical now.

Both Boleskine and the cellar have given me truly priceless experiences, which I can call upon during future SR work. Magic.

I was sent a message (May 2022), a piece from the Daily Record in Scotland saying Boleskine house is now open to the public. I take this as confirmation that my amazing SR teammates and I had completed all we were meant to, fantastic.

Ouija Boards

I HAVE COME to be made more aware of this type of instrument, which is used by people from all walks of life, from those who are trying to connect with loved ones to those practising dark magic.

I have done more SR work clearing places and homes with this as the main issue.

Anyone using this tool who does not know its full power or who does not know how to use it, or who does not have respect for what it can conjure up, can unknowingly create a very powerful negative space. This could be in a home or, as the dark forces have done, in nature, and this will allow entities and other forces to come in uninvited.

I would never use a Ouija board or anything similar, even though I have an idea of the power and chaos they can create. So please bear this in mind if someone you know tries to egg you on or tries to get you to become part of their gang. Ask yourself, 'Is it worth it?'

In my humble opinion, it's better to walk away than join in. Doing something you have no idea or little idea about will save you a lot of heartache. However, as with everything, it's your choice.

If you are curious, please seek guidance from someone such as me before doing anything connected to a Ouija board or anything similar. If you seek a message from a loved one perhaps try an Angel card reader or tarot reader, a medium or even try a natural healing therapy such as reiki, there is always a chance a message will come through the healer.

Then at least you will have some sort of understanding regarding the workings of such an item.

The Aleister Crowley SR ~ 3rd August 2016 to 15th October 2021

HAVING COMPLETED THE cellar SR, and rested for the next day or so, I was soon called upon by a soul who got my attention in a very vehement manner due to the coldness of his presence and his eagerness to connect with me and share his truth.

This was Aleister Crowley and, after some soul-searching, I accepted that my soul Shanti had played the role of Aleister as part of his journey.

As I relaxed in bed I called on my friends to oversee this SR because the visions I had received at the onset were a tad concerning, even for me, and even though I have done many SRs connected to the dark arts, as Aleister was.

These visions soon disintegrated, and I found myself relaxing into the understanding and the vibrational exchange of this part of my soul, who had connect to me during my first visit to Scotland. While on a tour of Scotland (circa 2016) I visited Loch Ness and parked up in St Augustus. I had a paddle in the Loch and then headed towards Boleskine without realising it. Thankfully, my guides got me to turn around before I arrived. I wasn't ready for that experience just yet. I was however, to connect with Aleister's essence, preparing me for my main visit. The trapped soul of Aleister finally connected to me while doing the SR at Boleskine, wow amazing.

Again, as the title of this book and my previous book suggest, souls or spirits use any means of transport possible to arrive at a specific place in time to make that connection, so I accept that this is how it was meant to be.

Also it's for me to trust that not everything is within the realms of logic. I must be open to all eventualities, and this is a prime example. Thank you, angels, for this insight.

Back to the SR.

Not knowing who it was, I began to talk to the soul. While finding out who it was it took me a little time to speak gently, as I felt guarded in some way. Perhaps I even felt a minute tremor of fear, but that soon dissipated as the chat moved along.

I first felt that this was part of my dad's soul and spoke in a way to forgive him, but this didn't resonate with me fully. Moments later I realised who it was and asked the question, 'Is Aleister a part of my soul?' I got the answer so definitively that I couldn't do anything but accept the answer as an unequivocal 'Yes.'

This shocked me for a moment. But then, as I went in a different direction with my questioning of Aleister,

I began to understand in greater depth why he had done the things he had.

As I become more in tune with the subtle differences energetically, I know that something had happened in his life, something to him or his loved ones that caused him to do the things he did. I felt that something had happened to his family, in particular to his mother.

Now I have spoken of the reptilians, who have been controlled by either the hierarchy of the reptilian race or by another off-world race even more than we humans have been.

With Aleister this is another such example. After what I believe to be some unpleasant threats towards his family he was given an ultimatum: do the work of the dark forces or see your family hurt or even executed.

This was not a pleasant situation to be in, so he chose reluctantly to do their work. He was initially a very powerful light worker.

Put yourself in his shoes, or indeed in those of any other person throughout history. Or even put yourself in any lifetime in which your soul has expressed to you in some way that they have done something unpleasant to others, and truthfully look inside yourself and see what you would have done in their situation. It is not an easy decision to make. Trust me, my soul has had this no-win situation occur many times over.

Would anyone want to see their loved ones tortured, indeed killed, if they could do anything to stop it?

Through my conversation with Aleister I came to understand his plight. In conjunction with his decision a reptilian was integrated into his being, but one who had been specifically programmed to control the vessel (Aleister's physical and mental well-being). Its aim was to focus on causing harm and programming the many others who became followers of the cult that Aleister formed. This almost eradicated the happy thoughts and memories that he had before this situation had occurred.

My voice softened during our chat, as I empathised with his plight. The SRs I have been blessed to be part of – helping our reptilian brothers and sisters, helping those who pass with dementia-type issues, clearing places where witchcraft or black magic has taken place, having the compassion to help those from other lifetimes that my soul has experienced such torture and pain with – are now an absolute honour for me to do.

It might be like hearing a stuck record, but I say again that we are all connected.
We are all one.
What I do unto others I do unto myself.

When we really understand these statements, we will never judge anyone ever again. I only know what I have experienced and what my soul releases through my physical body. I cannot and will not ever attempt to judge anyone who has succumbed to the dark side or whatever they have experienced. We do the best we can. Everyone does. We have always done the best we can in any given situation, with the knowledge we had at hand. And we always will.

The fact that our soul brings with it much wisdom and knowledge from its previous lifetimes gives us the opportunity to change the future here and now by learning from our soul and choosing to be kind rather than judging. This is the only way to ascend. This is what every soul who visits this planet sets out to accomplish. We are closer than ever to achieving this, but we can only do it when every soul has experienced all it came to experience. We can only ascend as one.

Anyway, back to the conclusion of this magical SR.

My questioning was now complete, so I spoke to this part of my soul, Aleister, to let go, to forgive and to forget about any type of revenge. These emotions are the ones that I had to release fully on behalf of this part of my soul before he could move on and swiftly return to connect with my soul, to help through his experiences. This balanced a lot of karma in the process.

I have been very tired today, Friday. As I type my eyes are becoming heavy, but I felt this needed writing about while it was still fresh in my mind. I am relieved and feel lighter for having had Aleister make himself known and having released all his excess baggage. Now I am in a much better place to be able to move forward with ease and grace to further assist in the helping of trapped souls everywhere so that they can be set free from the illusion they are trapped within.

This is my passion, this is my calling, and for this alone I am truly grateful.

Additional Information About Aleister Crowley

On 19th October 2021, during another epic healing at Yvonne's, I was given information about why I had kept getting a song called 'Secrets' in my mind quite repetitively over the last week or so.

This song was telling me what had happened in this lifetime, with my soul as Aleister. It was a secret he hid from his mother: the secret that he had turned from the angelic work he was doing to doing the work of the dark forces. He just couldn't bring himself to tell her. I feel that he was ashamed that he had allowed himself to be forced into something like that and couldn't bring himself to tell his mum.

I also want to speak about my first connection with the trapped soul of Aleister and my thoughts that it was my dad's soul. I have again been blessed with information that my angelic friends had me believe this to be true.

It was their magical way of helping me forgive, layer by layer.

Once I had forgiven what I had thought were Dad's actions, I was then able to forgive at a deeper level when receiving the truth that it was part of my soul who was here in the form of Aleister.

The "layer" scenario has happened many times but none more so than the Anonymous SR you will read about later in this book.

The Dr Zhivago SR ~ 17th October 2021

THIS LIFETIME HAS just been brought to my attention via a TV series called *New Tricks*. It is a detective series that looks at unsolved cases from the past. The episode in question highlights a couple trying to get away from Germany with their new-born child during WWII. The child was given to the Resistance and escaped but the man and woman had to stay behind. The woman told her partner to blow the whistle on her so she would be arrested, which would leave him free to search for their child in the future. This was a very tough decision to make, for the woman was killed for the attempted escape.

This has highlighted a lifetime that the title of this SR showed me when watching the film a few years ago, which brought so much emotion up for me via many tears. The film is set against a backdrop around the Russian Revolution, and I do believe that this is the same period as the lifetime I am writing about now took place. A true love story destined to fail.

The ending of the film sees a woman with her child. Knowing that she is about to be arrested and, more likely than not, killed, she tells the child to run. The child, who is around four years of age, doesn't know what's happening. He becomes very upset, but eventually does as his mum tells him. The woman lives in hope that by telling the child to run his father may seek to find him in the future.

Now this is the heartbreaker because in the final scenes, the woman and the child walk past a cafe. The father is in the cafe and sees the woman. He gets up and tries to get her attention but has a heart attack and dies. The woman and child walk past the cafe, oblivious to what has just happened there. So the child runs away with no chance of his father ever finding him, which leaves him abandoned and living a life full of torment.

This is what happened to my soul and the souls of my mum and dad in the Dr Zhivago-style life, and what emotions this has hidden for all three of us.

In the lifetime as the child, I didn't know the truth about why Mum did what she did. Thankfully the TV series showed me the truth behind it. I now know Mum had no choice. She felt this was the best way to save me, and by hoping my father was still alive it was her best option – whereas I, the child, felt abandoned. Had she realised that my father had passed, she may have made a different decision. But that's all hypothetical and of no importance here and now in this present lifetime.

Seeing the truth now has initiated a great release of emotional baggage for all the souls involved in this lifetime. And seeing the truth has dispelled the belief that my soul was abandoned. My soul has carried this for a long time.

It has helped me also realise that in the other lifetimes where my soul felt abandoned there may well have been a perfectly valid reason for my soul feeling that way. But as I look deeper into those lifetimes with stronger spiritual connections I can see how the wires could have become crossed and did become crossed. I understand, and with this understanding, forgiveness comes easier.

For Mum and Dad in that lifetime I now offer forgiveness to them both and I forgive myself for not knowing the truth, as I was just a child. Indeed, for all lifetime experiences surrounding this issue and the souls involved, I forgive us all.

Both Mum and Dad in that lifetime passed with deep regret for all that had gone on. I pray, as I have now seen the truth, that this will bring a blessed end for all involved, for the weight has been a heavy burden for each soul to carry.

They weren't married but were lovers. Their paths crossed at various points in this lifetime, but they were never able to be together as they wanted. They were like two ships passing in the night, but with a child connecting them. It just wasn't meant to be.

It really wasn't.

It was all part of our combined souls' journeys and it has just been put to bed, as once I had received this information I implemented the swiftest and most beautiful SR I have ever done.

After having shed a tear or two after resolving this

whole issue, mainly due to relief, I began to talk to the trapped parts of Mum and Dad's soul from this lifetime and to mine too. I called upon Archangel Azrael and him alone. It's all I felt I needed to do.

I have no idea how long they were with me and that part of my soul or where they connected to me, but that isn't important.

What is important is that I was able to instigate through SR their souls and that of my soul from that life being escorted into the light by Archangel Azrael. All three of them walked into the light hand in hand. It was so beautiful. And what a gift for each of them, to be blessed with the cleansing and clearing of this lifetime. This has had a great bearing on all our lives in this present lifetime, which I have only just been made aware of.

I add this SR because I feel this is a key lifetime, a key issue, which really will allow Mum, Dad's and my soul to move forward with greater ease. Wherever Mum and Dad's souls are at this moment, may they feel as light as mine does.

All three souls trapped in this life will now be taken to a realm by Archangel Azrael, where they will be blessed with healing and cleansing from this lifetime and be able to reconnect with the larger part of their souls, which will allow them to enjoy a better life experience somewhere else in time.

I send them so much love and thanks for all they have done for me and my soul. For me I feel the way this has come together today has again been orchestrated to perfection by my angelic friends. This is in part why our lives in this lifetime have played out as they have, to bring closure to this cycle, wow!

Thank you, thank you, thank you, so much.

The Swift SR ~ 21st October 2021

This morning I went to the seaside, Cleveleys again. While we were still in the full moon phase I thought, 'Where better to release any lingering attachments from the last few days?' It was very breezy yet sunny. Perfect conditions to blow the cobwebs away.

As I prepared to do my standing meditation I took a couple of photos, making sure – and I do mean making sure – that when I turned my back on the sea I was far enough away for not even a rogue wave to catch me unawares. The photos took a minute at most, yet my angelic friends thought it would be funny to catch me off guard despite my precautions. I looked down at my feet and saw they were surrounded by water. My feet, socks and trainers were wet. Aah, well. However, there was method in my angelic friends' madness regarding my feet getting wet, as I was soon to find out.

Having accepted this drenching I began a standing meditation, during which a lady came to see if I was OK. The lady must have seen me standing close to the water's edge for quite a few minutes. Perhaps thinking there was something wrong, she asked me as much, but

I said, 'Yes, I'm fine. I usually paddle in the water but not today.'

The lady and her pet stood with me but a few minutes, and we had a little chat and then parted company. I stood there a few minutes longer when my angelic friends caught me with another rogue wave. This time I took it to mean that it was time to leave.

My feet were getting cold, so I set off back to the car. I called at Crystal Aura, the crystal shop in Leyland, to pick up some leaflets that Jaime had kindly printed off for me. While there I started to feel quite annoyed and frustrated. It shocked me because I had had a lovely day thus far and nothing had happened to bring these emotions up in me. I thought nothing of it and drove home.

Around 2.30 p.m. I was feeling quite strange but had been guided to rest for a moment with a kyanite crystal on my stomach. After twenty minutes or so I felt a bit better. I did get the sense that I had connected with a trapped soul and asked if I had. I got a 'Yes,' and assumed it was at the crystal shop, but no. It was a soul connecting to me from the lady's pet dog. So I called my SR teammates to put in place whatever they chose to do to help this soul move on. This was completed in minutes, but I felt no better. Hmm.

Minutes later, when I was sitting facing my laptop, I could sense Saul and the other pure reptilians who have also graced me with their help in the last few days. It didn't occur to me that it was a reptilian sister who had attached itself to me from the lady. she was obviously at that point where she forced the reptilian out via her vibration raising.

My angelic friends are certainly giving me enough opportunities to break free from the logical aspect of my work. As I have said, I thought the soul came from the crystal shop. A logical thought but for the time the lady stood with me, it was enough for her to transfer the reptilian to me.

A lesson learnt, I hope.

Having understood this, I again asked my SR teammates to assist, and this time I completed the SR very quickly indeed. It has been such a positive experience and has shown me that since my healing with Yvonne on Tuesday my sensitivity has been honed considerably. Now I am able to swiftly sense foreign energies from trapped souls, attachments, entities etc.

Yes, it took almost three hours from the moment the lady came to see if I was OK to the final SR that helped our reptilian friend move on. Had this situation unravelled a few weeks ago it would have taken me a few days, simply because it would have taken me longer to become aware of the energies.

Having had this experience, I feel that anything similar regarding this type of SR will be done in even less time.

I didn't get the lady's name but wish to thank her for her concern, which was very heart-warming. But again it is an example of how our angels work to bring us into contact with those we need to, and at the perfect time. Also for me to be aware of my energetic level at all times.

Everything Is Energy

Now, when doing SR for reptilians and perhaps for other other-worldly beings, I do feel that there is and will be very subtle differences from the normal SRs for the trapped parts of our soul.

First I need to explain that we are and everything is made up of energy, even the most solid forms, such as things like rocks. I'm sure you can think of more, but for now I wish to keep it as simple as I can.

When our souls spend time on earth, enjoying the many experiences within a vessel or vehicle such as our bodies, be it human, animal, bird, fish, tree or anything else, the physical aspect is solid for this realm. Perhaps other worlds are similar, but for now I'm concentrating on Planet Earth.

Indeed, many things are created to be solid within this illusion here on earth. If nothing was deemed solid, we wouldn't be able to experience a great many things – for example, driving. If the steering wheel in the car wasn't seen to be solid we would have nothing to take hold of. It would be exactly like ghosts when they are depicted in films or in programmes when they flow through walls, unable to grasp or hold on to anything.

Around the time of my awakening in 2003 I was gifted some guidance. I'm not sure where I got it from, but I was to sit and softly stare into a mirror, focusing on a specific point on my face, and I was to keep practising until I had trained my focus to a point where I was sufficiently able to stare into the mirror to see my face change shape.

When I had been staring for a long time I'd see my face merging into other faces, and when I had achieved a level of softly staring into the mirror my face would disappear completely until I lost focus. Then my face would come back into view. It was quite scary at first, but it showed me that everything is energy. Even when focusing on what we would call a solid object it too would start to vibrate as my focus became stronger.

This took months to achieve.

I add this piece to help you see that everything is energy and fluid, even the most solid of structures. If you choose to try this, my humble guidance would be that you take baby steps all the way, and please stop at the first sign of any slight distress to your eyes.

So everything is energy, and I do mean everything.

Our souls can flit in and out of our bodies at will, whenever they chose, especially when our physical body rests or goes to sleep.

Our reptilian friends are also energy. However, their form is pure energy. They don't have a physical body, as we do. This is how they have appeared to me since our connection. It may well be different for others who have experiences with these angels.

When our physical body resonates at the frequency of fear or from fear-related issues, this gives the green light to the reptilian controllers to force or to coax our brainwashed friends into infiltrating the physical body. They will stay there until the physical body dies or achieves an energetic frequency higher than that of fear, which is enough to force the unwitting reptilian energy body out.

Therefore SR for our reptilian friends is slightly different. When they are evicted from the physical body they are stranded in limbo and await the pure reptilians, such as my guide Saul and others, to connect with them and to bring them to a place where they can be helped to move on.

The slight differences with the reptilians and with those whose souls pass with dementia-related issues make their SRs more challenging to complete.

The reptilians bring with them their programmed issues – the heavy energies of fear and chaos that their captors have instilled in them – which, until we become aware of them, can affect us greatly in negative ways.

This is a big part of the SRs for these beings, and so too for those with dementia-type issues. They will imprint upon us their state of mind, their deep fear, their confusion and their fragility. All these emotions and states can affect us.

Therefore I have gone to great lengths to share this information with you. And this is why I believe that the swift SR was a great experience for me to learn from, and how rapidly emotions can start to have an effect on us. As I have stated, it took me just three hours from the lady and the dog standing by my side near the sea to me realising that I needed to do a SR for a reptilian friend.

But in those three hours I had already started to feel a difference. The energies of frustration coming from our reptilian friend had started to infiltrate my energy field.

I can only share these divinely guided words because I have been blessed with the experiences of this SR, and previously I was also gifted a few hours of experiencing the symptoms of someone with dementia-type issues by my dad.

I state categorically my belief that all the trapped souls and beings I have written about in the previous few paragraphs reside within the closest reality to what I would call hell.

Dementia causes a person to flit from one realm to another at any given moment, thus causing great vulnerability. It also causes the person to experience such arduous challenges even with the seemingly easiest of tasks, which an able-minded person would do without even thinking.

My few hours of experiencing dementia-type symptoms were frightening, simply because I had no idea what was going to happen from one moment to the next.

When reptilians are ousted from their home the physical body they have resided in is left stranded in limbo, so they have no idea where they are or what to do. It could be compared to an extreme reality change – for example, a billionaire who has everything taken away from them in one fell swoop. It's as drastic a change as we can imagine.

I will give the dementia-type trapped souls, the

reptilians and any other similar universal beings who I may meet during my SR and EC work my full attention, as I do with every SR.

But I give even more to these groups of beautiful angels. I make doubly sure that I treat them with respect, comfort, compassion, understanding and so much love, for the experiences I have been gifted have blessed me with this empathy. It is without price.

The Revenge SR ~
1400s to 2nd November 2021

As I start to write, I have only the barest bones of information at hand. I have been asked by my SR teammates to trust them more, so here goes.

It revolves around the issue of revenge and how both my soul and yours have experienced this during our many differing lifetimes here on earth.

This issue began in the 1400s.

The situation that evolved had my soul's physical body seeking revenge for things done to him. My soul's physical body waited patiently for many years to see his plans for revenge come to fruition.

My soul in that lifetime was imprisoned unjustly. What made it worse was the fact that he knew things about his captor that, if they ever got out, would harm the person markedly. He was also impeded by the addition of a face mask that not only covered his face but also an added implement on the mask entered his mouth, which prevented my soul's physical mouth from speaking for the duration of this internment.

As the years passed the feeling of vengefulness

multiplied. The more it consumed him the more he became paranoid, until one day it finally manifested into his reality and for the person who had the restraint fitted. I'm being shown that he was a patron of the church at that time. I haven't been shown what my soul's physical body did to the perpetrator, but I can hazard a guess that it wasn't pleasant, so there's obviously no need for me to know. Which is fine.

Over the years this ate away at my soul's physical body like a cancer, until the day came when he fortuitously escaped and was finally able to put his plan of revenge into action. You would think that my soul's physical body would have been overjoyed at the successful culmination of a vendetta lasting almost a lifetime against one man.

Well, you would be wrong, so wrong, as I too have come to understand.

All the while he was awaiting his opportunity, my soul's physical body kept going over and over the feelings of deep satisfaction that he would experience when achieving his goal, which built his excitement up no end. But this was not to be the case.

Now this lifetime, the cycle that was to be ended and the SR itself, were brought to me in stages.

The first stage occurred in 1999 when I foolishly became involved in a dispute, during which I came off worse and spent two weeks in hospital. While at the time this situation was unpleasant for my family as well as for me, many blessings have since come from it. These positives are what I focus on now.

The second stage occurred a few years ago, when visiting Lancaster Castle with a few friends to take in the tour and to connect to the part of my soul that was trapped there. I wasn't aware of this connection until a few days ago.

There was a room with different types of masks from a period in history that includes the one I'm writing about now. However, when seeing the masks my reaction was an alarming one. Seeing them brought the memory back, and sharpish too. No wonder I had a slight fear about masks covering my face.

The next stage came when I was guided to watch two films: *Now You See Me* and *Now You See Me 2*. Both films were based around magic, but held within them was a complex and well-thought-out plot to seek revenge.

In the first film a police officer, seeking revenge for the death of his father, succeeded in the final scene, and saw the man he had targeted and set up for over thirty years finally behind bars as part of his intricate plan.

In the second film the officer, having successfully taken his revenge in the first film, had to then seek the help of the man who he had imprisoned to help him locate four magicians who were in danger and who had been brought together under the officer's tutelage to set up an unscrupulous businessman and his son. He was an officer but was also a member of a secret magical group called the Eye, who selected targets to bring them to justice.

During a scene on a plane, the man imprisoned by the officer could see in the officer's eyes that the revenge he sought was nothing like he had expected.

This the officer denied fervently. This scene more than any other brought up this memory of my soul's past life and how that played out, which was very similar to the films in some respects.

I have just had a break and made a cuppa, and while doing so I felt the need to ask my guides a question. 'Am I doing the SR as I write?' I received a 'Yes.' I also asked, 'Is the trapped soul from this lifetime the cause for my unpleasant experiences over the weekend?' Again I got a 'Yes.'

So the trapped soul had only just made himself known to me over the weekend. This makes so much sense now that I feel very relieved indeed. The emotions I have experienced over the weekend have been very destructive, in the sense that my soul's physical body had focused so much on seeking revenge in this lifetime that he had become paranoid due to his single-mindedness. I felt the disappointment and the emptiness of the failed outcome that my soul's physical body had created through his numerous thoughts about how his revenge would play out and the feelings of satisfaction he would bask in, and finally how he felt cheated out of his joyful celebrations.

Expectation of any kind can lead to disappointment if the expectation doesn't come to fruition the way we want it to. No wonder I felt very strange over the weekend, but this was showing me what I was being asked to release on behalf of my soul at this time. Now, after having obtained most of the jigsaw pieces regarding this lifetime, I can now begin to explain this situation to the trapped part of my soul from this lifetime.

I explained why he felt the outcome would be the

way he had expected but then found out that the result was drastically different than he thought. After accepting my words as truth he reluctantly let go and forgave the person's soul involved. By the time I finish this piece of writing he will be long gone, off into the light that my SR teammates have lovingly created. This SR was completed swiftly.

It has been one massive weight lifted from my shoulders, so I can only assume that the weight of the expectation, the disappointment, and feeling cheated, certainly all weighed heavily upon my soul's physical body too.

It must have been a massive let-down for my soul's physical body when, on realising what the outcome was, it hadn't exceeded his expectations. And, to make matters worse, he had accrued a great deal of karma through his thoughts, intentions and actions when the opportunity arose.

I now feel this added to my emotional and mental discomfort during the weekend. It's making so much sense now.

These are the emotions that I was blessed with. I needed to have felt them in advance of the SR, so that I was able to fully let go of the emotions that surfaced for me to release before being called upon to do this SR. The bonus is that I have been blessed with further knowledge to call upon when I do other SR work involving the issue of revenge.

I can say these things without doubt:
1. Seeking revenge is something I will never do again, no matter what happens.

2. Some say revenge is a dish best served cold.
3. I say that revenge is a dish to be taken off the menu, period.

The outcome was that my soul's physical body was caught for the actions taken against the man of the cloth and was sentenced to a term in Lancaster Castle. He never saw the light of day again. That is why my soul was trapped there.

By not retaliating or seeking revenge after the incident in 1999 I have brought the cycle to an end without even knowing it until now. This has set my soul free and has also set free the soul of the person who was involved in the incident in 1999.

Our souls have finally got off the roundabout through my actions, or the non-action that I subconsciously chose just after the incident happened. I also asked his soul to forgive my actions too, because both souls involved have experienced both roles as the perpetrator and the victim many times.

Some may feel I have been a coward, or that I have let the person off the hook, or anything else that anyone may think of. In the past, before understanding this spiritual path, I may have agreed with you. But now I know the damage that retaliating to a situation or seeking revenge for something done to my soul and the various physical bodies it has resided within throughout this cycle and those close family and friends in those lifetimes too, I would no longer agree. And the same can be said of the other soul involved.

Somewhere along the journey one soul must take the lead and be the bigger person, to set in motion the ending of any cycle that they have been entangled in.

My soul and the other person's soul have created an avalanche of karma for themselves, as we experienced physical pain and trauma. For example, in my case I am still releasing from the broken cheekbone sustained in the 1999 incident. The mental and emotional turmoil both souls have experienced have also taken their toll.

So by not seeking revenge I have set my soul free and the other person's too, which I am so glad to have been able to do through my spiritual understanding.

Had we stayed on the roundabout, more pain and trauma would be experienced on both sides, but at what cost?

Yes, the experience in this lifetime with me ending up in hospital caused me great trauma. Mum and Dad suffered greatly too, but because I have refused to seek revenge I have ended this cycle once and for all. To know that no one else will suffer from this part of my soul's journey is worth so much more than seeking revenge. The extra piece of information I have just received is that the soul of the man in this present lifetime's experience, has been the one in many lifetimes, the SR I have written about included.

I will say it again: we are all connected, we are all one.

What I and my soul have caused others during a myriad of lifetimes experiences I did unto myself.

I now choose peace, love and forgiveness.

Choosing this path takes strength and not weakness, as some see it.

It's the only way to move forward in life.

The Abandonment SR ~ Date Unknown to 3rd November 2021

I HAVE WRITTEN about this issue vaguely in the odd piece of writing in various ways since I began to write. However, today I can, with the help of many angels and the souls of my mum and dad, bring this cycle to an end.

My soul has been on a journey, experiencing abandonment in one form or another, mainly connected to Mum's soul in this lifetime. Her soul has been my mother in many other incarnations, just as my dad's soul has been my father in many other incarnations. In truth it had to be this way until the awareness came through to me to be able to forgive, to understand and to thoroughly end this cycle once and for all.

I have just watched a TV programme in which the child of a couple was thought to have been kidnapped or worse, only for the truth to come out that the father knew he wasn't the father of the child. When he found out who the real father was he promptly arranged for him to take guardianship of the child, whereas the mother was left to believe that the child was dead. The father obviously didn't want to raise a child who wasn't his own.

This highlights just another way our combined souls (Mum's, Dad's and mine) have experienced this issue in different lifetimes. I have written about one way in the Dr Zhivago SR. This is another way we experienced this issue to finally help me see the truth, after having done the spiritual work necessary to understand everyone's position in their varied roles in the various lifetimes.

Now I can offer forgiveness to everyone involved, including myself, for getting the wires crossed. I thought that Mum was leaving me, abandoning me. In truth I thought that she didn't love me. This is the core issue. The many ways that our souls have experienced this issue had imprinted on my soul that I wasn't loved.

This is another crossed wire that I have nurtured in this lifetime since Mum passed in 2005. Now I still do feel the emotions I felt when Mum passed. Those feelings surfaced again: the being left behind, abandoned, unloved. These emotions could only have been brought up by my mum's soul. It was the only way of ensuring that a complete release of all unhealthy emotions and feelings attached to this issue could be obtained.

However, it helps me understand why I felt life to be so hard when Mum passed or left in this and other lifetimes. It helps me understand that this cycle needs to be broken in a way so that in the future I enjoy life rather than allow everything to spiral downwards.

While we are all connected, I do believe that some soul connections for this experience here on earth are stronger than others. This connection with Mum's soul is one of the strongest, if not the strongest.

I have written about ending cycles, included in the pages of the previous SR, with the help of the experiences that I have had to become aware of in order to help bring these cycles to an end. This is another of those cycles. When Mum passed in 2005, I had no idea this was another opportunity for my soul to break free of the spiralling downwards when I believed that I had been abandoned by Mum's soul, which had happened in every other lifetime thus far. It makes so much sense now.

When Mum passed in 2005, I had no idea how I would survive without her. I didn't get on with Dad, but this too was a blessing in disguise. I now understand why my feelings about Dad in this lifetime weren't the most loving ones. It is because his soul has played the villain in this cycle, which has run the course of many lifetimes. Our souls have had much karma to balance from many lifetimes past. This could only be achieved by Mum passing in this lifetime first, which gave Dad and me and our souls the opportunity to heal the rift and to uncross the many crossed wires, which during these many lifetimes have accrued negative feelings towards one another.

This rift and this cycle have been brought to my attention today and I thank the universe and every angel within it for this blessed feeling of relief, not only for our souls (Dad's and mine) to have the karma balanced, but for my ancestors too. For they will be feeling the benefit of my awareness and understanding and knowing I will act positively regarding the rift and the cycle, rather than seeking any sort of revenge, which my soul has done over the long duration of this issue. But now we forgive, to end this cycle, so we can all move on and leave all this behind us.

I needed to understand how and why everything had happened in this life. Being prepared for a day such as this, which brought the curtain down on this issue, is truly humbling, particularly regarding how it has been choreographed in such complex ways, yet with every moment and every experience in divine order.

To my angelic friends from all realms, you never cease to amaze me. Thank you for your guidance, help, love and wisdom. To now feel the way I feel is truly priceless.

I almost forgot... The SR for Mum, Dad and my trapped souls from any number of lifetimes involved with this abandonment issue meant that they too have now moved on with ease. Again I write these precious words down.

This is my and Shanti's challenge here and now, for in every other lifetime this scene has been played out: the ending of my soul's physical life has been full of despair, pain and loneliness.

Only today, as this awareness came to my attention, have I realised that I must do this from here on in. I must enjoy life, not beat myself up. It really makes so much sense now and gives Shanti and me a new start, a new beginning, from which to change our direction in life and to enjoy and to love life without any feelings of guilt or anger.

I have been subconsciously carrying this burden on my shoulders since Mum passed in 2005 and since the duration of this issue, whenever it began.

What a weight I can now let go of – without too much discomfort please, angels.

All this is coming to fruition on the eve of the new moon, which is coming in on 4th November and just as we exited the Mercury retrograde phase at 1 a.m. this morning, 3rd November.

Is this is coincidence?
No way.
Everything is in divine and perfect order.
Always.

The Night of a Thousand SRs ~ 15th & 16th November 2021

THIS VERY BUSY period, from the evening through to the morning, has been a truly amazing experience, with many SRs being done. Hence the title of this piece.

SR 1

I was reminded about a SR that we started when driving around a small area near Chorley in Lancashire the other day. I was unable to physically walk around the area as it was fenced off. Having received this reminder, I began this SR by inviting my teammates to play their part while I slept. My soul needed to be at the site to help clear and close the portal that had been opened, again by a group of people using spiritual tools without knowing the power within them. This is becoming a regular occurrence in the SRs we as a team are doing currently.

A Ouija board, among other tools, was being used. Unbeknownst to the users it had, through their actions, invited other-worldly beings from the dark side to enter earth. Thankfully this is what we as a SR team dealt with this morning. Once the portal was closed any souls trapped there were set free, and the whole area was blessed with a deep energetic cleansing. So all the negativity that had built up over the centuries was now cleared.

And that was just the start.

SR 2

While I slept the above SR was completed. On waking during the night I was given information that another SR was to be done. This involved a recent SR that I had done for the town where I was born, Leigh.

I was shown the canal I walked along and the area I walked into under a bridge, where dodgy dealings were going on. I felt like I was walking into the lion's den. My only thought when I realised what I had walked into was, 'Run, Jeffrey, run.'

Archangel Michael made himself known and calmly guided me to walk away rather than run. This I managed to do, but it was a challenge.

So the next SR was to clear the areas where my soul had experienced unpleasant situations where I had run away. When I say *run away*, I mean I had run away from situations that would have caused my physical body great harm, even death. By running away, in those lifetimes, others viewed my actions as being cowardly. Others felt I had betrayed them by leaving them to face the music.

So within this SR all these situations were blessed with peace and balanced for all the souls involved, and all parts of my soul were set free from many an unpleasant experience.

SR 3

I went back to sleep, only to awake a few hours later with more information and another SR about to begin. The information I received involved no. 158, the house I had lived in with Mum and Dad for many a year. I was shown that my mum's, my dad's and my soul had lived in this house prior to the lifetime I have written about extensively.

The life I was now being shown was in the 1950s, and the physical bodies who lived there were playing out a similar lifetime to the one that Mum, Dad and I have had in this lifetime. I saw that in this previous life in the 1950s that some cycles were not completed, and that my parents again returned to live in this house from 1964 in different physical bodies. They were given the opportunity to complete the lessons that had so far been left unfinished.

You may sense or experience this where you live now or, if you move, at your new address. There is a reason for this. Just as my family and I returned to the same house in the future, so too will your soul guide you to live in the same area or even the same house to complete unfinished business if needs be.

I have done SRs for people whose souls had resided within those houses in a previous lifetime – not all of them, but some. This was another timely reminder for me. This time it was more of an EC with some SR done too, for my soul had become trapped in the 1950s as well as being trapped in this recent lifetime. So two parts of my soul had been trapped in the same house.

SR 4

Having invited my SR teammates to again do what they could to bring this to a magical conclusion, I went back to sleep. While sleeping I was shown a vision of a large hill or a mountain with cable cars coming down from the summit.

I was also in a house chatting with a family. I had no idea what about, but when I woke up I felt a little emotional in a very good way and had the word *shekel* ringing in my ears. I looked up what a shekel was and soon felt that this word was a sign about where this astral travel had taken me to. It was Israel.

During the afternoon I was blessed with more information regarding this visitation. This helped to clear up another lifetime that had caused my soul a great deal of mental, emotional and physical pain. I didn't see this bit, but I was taken to where my wife and daughter had been slaughtered, where their souls were finally set free via a SR. I wasn't given a time period for this lifetime, but it was quite a long time ago. And it seems to have had a great bearing on all my later lifetimes until now.

All this and it wasn't even 9 a.m. When eventually I woke I felt so tired, but much lighter. Much work had been done over the last few hours. I am now writing this piece in the afternoon, having enjoyed a quiet day preparing myself and bringing myself into alignment with my writing angels. This is to make sure that, as with all the pieces of writing I do, they are truthful. It is so important that I trust my angelic friends and my sacred heart, rather than doing research. I'm being guided to trust that what I feel to resonate within me is my truth. I'm doing my best.

And now it really is time for me to rest and to allow the healing that has occurred to enter every cell of my being to further enhance my life from here on in.

Thank you, angels. I love you all so much.

The Massage Bed SR ~ 22nd & 23rd November 2021

THIS WAS A very interesting SR, which offered me a slightly new twist on SR work and how trapped souls make their way to the one who can help them.

I have written about a dog coming from Poland with part of my soul and I have written about a lady visiting a crystal shop and transferring part of her trapped soul into a crystal while visiting the shop. This is a similar situation, but it involves a massage bed.

On behalf of a friend I picked a massage bed up from another friend who had put it up for sale on Facebook yesterday, 22nd November.

I half-sensed that something was happening last night but didn't delve into it as I had other issues to deal with first.

I went to the seaside again today to be cleansed by the energies of the sea and nature, but only now do I see that my time there was clearing the way for this SR to be attended to now, in the afternoon, having returned triumphantly from the seaside.

This brought about the ending of a deeply emotional SR connected to another dear friend that began on

Sunday. However, this type of SR has been catalogued in previous SRs, so I won't go into too much detail about it. I will only say that it has brought up deep emotions within me to release. The Brucie Bonus for me was a timely reminder from my SR teammates that the emotions which surfaced were the emotions that my soul's physical body in that specific life had buried deep within his being. Only now could they be released, and with great effect too. This is the only slight difference in this SR. Everything else revolved around family life and an unpleasant ending.

So back to the massage bed SR. The friend in question, Jane (an alias) and I connected via a group on Facebook, which now seems amazing because I only stayed in the group for a day. Let's just say that it wasn't my cup of tea.

I followed my guidance to perfection, which was to connect with Jane and then leave the group. The initial connection happened about four to five months ago. The massage bed was put up for sale by Jane. Another friend was looking for a massage bed. I shared Jane's post about the sale of the bed. These factors all contributed to me meeting up with Jane to take receipt of the bed after having a very brief chat while finalising the transaction.

I have no idea how long the soul had been embedded in the massage bed, but in part it knew what it needed to do to get relief from the illusion it was trapped in, by finding its way to me.

So as I write I now sense that the soul is part of Jane's soul and it has a connection with my soul. It obviously made its way to me to bring a gentle yet loving conclusion to the other life experiences that these two souls shared. Our souls, Jane's and mine, have probably had more experiences than this one, but for that information to come through I will have to be patient. 'One SR at a time,' my guides are telling me.

The Anonymous SR ~ from BCE to 18th January 2022

I FEEL THAT the title of this SR is self-explanatory. The experiences of these lifetimes are to be kept private for now. But I will share with you how very challenging a situation it has been since being first introduced to this other lifetime, which has caused me great heartache throughout.

I was made aware of this lifetime over ten years ago now, via another healing session with Yvonne where the lords of karma came in and began to unravel the bandages that covered my whole body. This was symbolic because this was the lifetime in question being karmically balanced, which set me free during this process. This was a beautiful and magical gift, but little did I know that this would just be the beginning of a very troublesome lifetime to accept and to forgive myself for. And for me to release the emotions and mental torture from the physical body that Shanti, my soul resided in at this time.

It was a lifetime that my soul agreed to play a particular role but had no idea of the consequences until the lords of karma blessed me with the removal of the bandages. They instigated the real healing process, and I hope that writing about this now will bring down the curtain on this lifetime once and for all.

My angelic friends blessed me with information this morning, 29th November 2021, which opened my awareness to the magnitude of the intricately created layers that were shown to me at the right time so I could understand and know what was being asked of me. At the same time I had to be careful not to overload my physical body with the details of this lifetime, in which there have been many subtle layers.

Each time my angelic friends revealed another layer to this lifetime it took me all my strength to accept and release what was needed. A lack of self-worth, feelings of betrayal, shame, utter despair, a lack of forgiveness towards myself and other emotions would pour forth each time new information came to me, but each time I have had such immense support to help me survive these challenging times.

It has taken me many years to accept that what my soul experienced was everything it had signed up to experience. My soul did exactly what was asked of him, but that lifetime has been so challenging for me to accept and to forgive myself about because of the event that was taking place at the time due to the intense feelings which kept surfacing. Thankfully I hope we have now arrived at the point where I can fully forgive and accept what my soul did and caused, knowing that the other souls involved have already forgiven my soul. Indeed, they have thanked my soul for playing the role he played, but it has taken me so long to come to terms with this. However challenging it has been I now feel so blessed that my soul took on a role no other soul would, and that there have been many blessings coming from this lifetime.

To have conquered this lifetime here and now through much healing, where various SRs have taken place over the years, is a big relief. For I was very concerned why my life was always seemingly coming to a roadblock just when I had started to get somewhere. Fully understanding this lifetime and its experiences has now helped me surrender and let go completely, this is the greatest blessing of all.

I want to thank all those souls involved within this lifetime that I have written about here. Who knows, there may come a time when I speak about this lifetime freely, but for now I will keep it safely under wraps.

It is the morning of 18th January 2022.

I awaken to an energy, a trapped soul making itself known. This was not directly regarding a SR, but in the goodness of time I was to implement and call upon my SR teammates to do what I believe to be the most important SR thus far on a personal basis.

The trapped soul's main body came to enlighten me about what was going to happen, being supported throughout the uncomfortable SR that I and my SR teammates were invited to do. I felt quite a burden on my shoulders as I became increasingly aware of what was happening. I didn't want to let anyone down, especially the soul who came to guide and support me.

I did as I always do. It's almost automatic now. When talking to any soul who is trapped in some unpleasant illusion, as this soul was, it took me a lot of effort to stay balanced and calm and to trust that what I was saying and doing was perfect.

This is a real challenge. I came to understand that while the lifetime I have touched upon was filled with such negativity, what happened next helped me truly believe that things had been balanced. And it was so important for me to really and truly believe this.

People can say to us that it wasn't our fault, or that we did our best. Or they can say, 'Don't beat yourself up. Don't be embarrassed.' But until a time and a situation occur that help us to believe and trust these words for ourselves, what they say can often fall on deaf ears.

As I have said many times, everything happens within the realms of divine timing. And, as always, this experience is another prime example of this fact.

Only after having completed the SR did I fully realise that only then was I worthy enough – ready enough – to do this work on behalf of this trapped soul and its main soul body. I had reached an adequate level of self-worth.

The soul of this person who I shared this lifetime's experience with showed me that by helping his soul reunite via SR it was karma being balanced. It was God's way or the universe's way of giving me an opportunity to bring closure to this lifetime. I now understood everything that my soul's physical body in this lifetime had caused through his actions, and I was aware of the roles played by me and Shanti. Bringing these two soul particles back together has redressed the balance.

For the first time since this lifetime was made known to me over fourteen years ago do I feel fully at peace, knowing within my heart that everything has been balanced and that I can finally stop beating myself up.

To feel the relief and peace as I write this down is truly priceless. No amount of money could buy this experience, which stemmed from a challenging beginning but finished with a mind-blowing, magical ending.

I really do feel so blessed and utterly gobsmacked regarding how this lifetime has revealed itself over a period and that I obtained this conclusion, which I would never have thought possible until now.

I thank every angel involved with this amazing experience.

The Footballer's SR ~ from 26th to 29th November 2021

YESTERDAY I WATCHED a programme about a footballer who committed suicide a few years ago. After the programme had finished, I felt the trapped soul of this footballer was with me, so I called out his name. And, sure enough, the energetic change around me was so strong that I was in no doubt that he was here with me.

During our chat I asked how he connected with me. Instantly I was reminded of the fact that I had gone to the cinema on Friday to watch the latest James Bond film. On my way there I asked my SR friends to instigate anything they desired, be it a SR or an essence clearing or, as it turned out, to connect me and this footballer while I was in the vicinity.

Now it transpired that the footballer had challenging issues. In certain moments they would push him deep into depression and cause him to do things he would never have thought of otherwise, such was the seriousness of these bouts of depression. I have experienced this with Dad and his situation, due to the dementia-type illness he had.

The thing that resonated with me more than anything else was the fact that the footballer did set in motion the suicide via hanging himself, but at the last moment he had a change of heart (this was exactly what my soul experienced in another lifetime). Alas, the sequence of events could not be stopped because the footballer was alone, as was my soul's physical body, so there was no one to help by cutting us down from the rope. What a very tragic way to go.

I spoke to the footballer and, while inviting my SR friends to take care of this beautiful soul, I also asked them if they could bring all the souls involved and their higher selves together so the footballer could explain to his family what had happened. They obviously thought it was their fault because of something that they had done, when in truth it had nothing to do with any of them. This was the message that the footballer wanted to get through to his loved ones.

I sincerely hope this occurs in the future and that his family get some sort of closure however it may transpire. My wish is that his family do get to hear the truth about his death. For it will give them closure but more importantly it will give them a beginning from which to forgive themselves for whatever they thought the reason was behind this tragedy. And they will also be able to forgive the footballer for his actions.

Unless you can see the through the footballer's eyes it's hard to comprehend why someone would do such a thing. I again learnt this invaluable lesson from Dad. At first I hated Dad for trying to kill himself, but over time I came to forgive him and truly respect him for his actions and why he did what he tried to do. In my eyes it takes great courage to attempt suicide, even if it is a cry for help. The person doing this is obviously in great distress and feels that this is the only way to get help. Or they may go through with it and succeed.

It will be the lesson of the footballer's family to forgive him and to see the blessings held within his seemingly untimely departure.

Our soul is on a journey, and it will leave any physical body when it is time to do so. It doesn't hang around until there's a right time for it to leave, because there is never a right time for us as humans to understand. The soul is everlasting and is on a constant voyage of discovery of who it truly is, especially when experiencing this wonderful earth experience.

To realise that there is no such thing as loss is one of humanity's greatest lessons. This is one of earth's greatest gifts for our souls to experience while we reside here.

The Soulmate SR ~ from BCE to 8th December 2021

THIS SR HAS been one where it has taken a few years for the information to come through so that I would be able to complete it for my soul and for those involved.

Last week while at the seaside I knew it was necessary for me to stand in the water for however long was necessary, even though it was a very cold day and the water was almost at freezing point. As I walked towards the sea barefoot my feet were almost turning blue with each step, such was the cold, but standing in the sea was a must. I stood in the water for around three minutes, but that was enough. I hurriedly walked to the promenade and sat down while warming my feet up by putting my socks and shoes back on.

As I left I had no idea what had taken place and thought no more about it until I started to feel very cold all the way down my left side at various times throughout the day and over the next few days. This started on Tuesday 30th November, a day after my seaside experience. Luckily I had been contacted by Yvonne, offering me an appointment for a healing that Friday, so I hadn't long to wait for the answers I sought. I did ask repeatedly for answers, but none were forthcoming. I was asked to trust that everything would be made known to me at the perfect time.

My healing session with Yvonne was, as always, filled with many blessings. I did ask Yvonne if she saw any souls with me that were causing this intense cold feeling down my left side. Before the main healing took place Yvonne said that she couldn't see anything, but afterwards she told me what had happened.

Yvonne went into another lifetime where my soul's physical body lived in the Himalayas. He and his true love were walking across a body of water that had frozen over but not hard enough to take the weight of both their bodies. Yvonne went on to say that my soul's true love fell in. He tried to pull her out but couldn't. Yvonne's last message told of my true love going with the flow of water under the ice.

As this lifetime moved on my soul's physical body became a monk who took a vow of celibacy. He went off into the mountains to be alone and spent years in a cave, where he had almost no connection with the outside world until passing in the cave due to the freezing conditions and, most likely, a broken heart.

After the main healing Yvonne said that his true love's name was Annika and that she was standing by her side, dripping with water.

This was the reason for the coldness down my left side. Having been unable to save Annika from drowning, my soul's physical body lay on the ground for some considerable time, trying in hopeless desperation to save her. After a while he felt only utter despair after realising she had gone.

Now there are a few things that needed to be attended to having received this information.

First: the vow of celibacy needed to be broken.

Second: I was shown where my fear of needing closure had surfaced in other lifetimes, including this present one. When Dad passed my first action was to make sure that it was Dad lying on the floor and that he had passed.

Third: the guilt I had felt in this lifetime and in others needed to be fully let go of.

Fourth: I was gifted another magical way that souls connect with us.

I hadn't really thought of souls using the waterways of the world and the oceanic angels to help a trapped soul arrive at a destination at the perfect time to connect with me, as Annika's did just a few days ago. I did however experience this in the Pictish SR via mermaids but had forgotten about it until now. This is another example of how profound the title of these two *Taxi for 'Spirit'* books is.

Now I thought the SR had been concluded while at Yvonne's, but that was not the case. Instead I was to bring the curtain down on this amazing SR yesterday evening, 5th December 2021.

I again felt the coldness return to my left side, but with a subtle difference. It was Annika making herself known to me, and through a knowingness I felt she was there to help my soul, which was trapped in the cave while freezing to death. I had done some work a good few years ago on this part of my soul's life living in the cave but had now been blessed with the full story. My soul Shanti had, for one night as I slept, ventured to the cave to bring this part of my soul home and had quietly stayed hidden until this time, mostly because of the guilt he felt.

Therefore the SR was to be concluded here at home and in private. Annika was telling me that it was her time to go and for my soul and me to let go of the guilt.

The SR was concluded very quickly with the help of Archangel Azrael. As I write this piece, my knees down to my feet are freezing. This took a little while to come through, but this is the trapped soul of a wolf who had befriended my soul's physical body when living and meditating in the cave who stayed by his side until the wolf also passed.

This is a SR I feel so honoured to have done because of the friendship and loyalty this beautiful soul had shown.

It's now 8th December 2021. As I write, I am bringing a cycle to an end much bigger than I ever thought since this lifetime came up during the healing.

I have today been made aware that Annika's soul is the same soul who was my mum in this present lifetime. She has either been my daughter, sister, mother or lover in each of the incarnations that had been created for my soul to finally break this cycle. This scenario has spanned many lifetimes in many ways, but each has gifted my soul's physical body in any given lifetime the opportunity to bring this cycle to an end.

> The cycle is the loss of my soulmate.

In each lifetime Mum's soul, in whatever guise – be it my sister, my mum or whoever she might be – left before mine, so that my soul had an opportunity to conquer the fear of not being able to live without her. This is very true about this present lifetime too.

I came close to ending it all after Mum's passing in 2005, but thankfully something stopped me from even attempting suicide this time around, although it has been a tough period to get through since Mum passed. In each lifetime, as in this present one, I was left alone after Mum's soul had moved on and I never recovered from the loss. Each lifetime ended with my soul's physical body succeeding in committing suicide in various ways.

So my challenge, should I accept it, is this: I am hoping that by finally completing this SR and severing the cords of the unhealthy attachment to Mum's soul, I will have done all I can to give myself the best opportunity to enjoy life and to end this lifetime in a natural way. In those lifetimes I have literally sacrificed myself each time.

This must end this time.

This information is the piece that completes this deeply emotional jigsaw. As I sat writing this piece the other day the emotion that surprisingly didn't materialise during the healing came out very forcibly, but I immediately stopped the flow and stopped writing.

I now know that I wasn't ready to let go of the unhealthy attachment to my mum's soul. Things have transpired over the last two days to keep me isolated and still until this morning, when I began to accept the information coming to me about Mum's soul being Annika and what I needed to do to set free these two souls.

It took a few days to also realise that the soul who played the role of Annika had to be a very strong soul connection, maybe even the strongest. Hence this is the reason why I needed to do a second SR today for the trapped part of my soul who didn't want to move on the first time. Thankfully he has today.

The Ardlui & Loch Lomond SR ~ from July 2017 to 17th December 2021

THIS SR BEGAN to raise its head after a quick chat on Messenger with Yvonne last Sunday and a seemingly innocuous statement she made, which triggered all sorts of conflict within me.

The statement was this: 'I was wondering if we should go to Lilford to complete the cycle.'

This related to 21st December, the winter solstice, and where we would go to perform our ritual. It took me a while to reply, and all the while my stomach was doing somersaults. There was something amiss there. It has taken a few days for it all to unravel, but today it has.

I was feeling nothing regarding going to Lilford Park to do the ritual. I had had this feeling before, a few months ago, when a full moon ritual was coming up. It took me a while to gain the courage to tell Yvonne that I wasn't going because I felt drawn to the sea.

This is exactly how I felt when reading this statement. But how should I tell Yvonne? The last time the blow was cushioned by the fact that Yvonne and the others had to cancel the Lilford ritual because of bad weather, so knowing this had helped lessen my guilty feelings about going to the seaside on that occasion.

This time the feelings of guilt about letting Yvonne down and feeling I was betraying her were a little too much. This all happened on Sunday 12th December. And, strangely, it was just after my visit to the sea again to do the 12/12 gateway anchoring of the energies coming in on this auspicious day.

The day after I went to Rivington for a walk to see if I could get some clarity on this situation. I did, but it really rattled me. I was standing by a small waterfall feeling the vibration of the water as it cascaded down the hill. I had only just settled after closing my eyes and focusing on the sounds of the water when a few moments later a dog started to bark, and boy did it shock me. I was so deep in meditation that I didn't know where I was. The bark had certainly brought up the fear that had been so deeply ingrained within me it that I needed some shock treatment.

I composed myself and went about my walk. Nothing surfaced information-wise until this morning, Wednesday 15th December, when I woke early and was drawn to visit the sea yet again. This time the information would flow easily and clearly.

The feelings I had pertained to a lifetime with Yvonne's soul and mine enjoying a romantic lifetime. This is the first lifetime of a romantic nature I can remember that we have delved into during many, many healing sessions with Yvonne. However, having cleared the cycle with my mum's soul in the previous SR, it makes perfect sense now. Now it was time to complete this cycle, the cycle of those lifetimes where Yvonne's soul and mine have experienced romance – albeit ending in tragedy, as this lifetime shows.

I was reminded about a tour of Scotland I did in 2016 after Dad had passed earlier the same year. I visited various places that Dad and Mum had visited and loved. I also visited some places that I was drawn to visit for my soul's journey. All told, they were a very emotional few weeks.

On the way down the west coast I felt drawn to visit Loch Lomond and came across a place called Ardlui. I stayed in the Ardlui Hotel for a night. Now Mum's name was Louie, so after seeing this sign I had to stay, didn't I?

Ardlui was so very apt. Mum's name was Louie, and her life was so very h(Ard): Ardlui... How our angelic friends work.

I spoke to the lady on reception and got talking about what I do, including working with angels. The lady mentioned that they had had some strange experiences in Room 18. I said, 'Would you like me to see what I can pick up?' The lady said 'Yes,' and led me up the stairs to Room 18, which was on the way to my room in the attic.

I didn't feel too much, but got the overpowering smell of cherry. It didn't seem important at the time, but now as I write this piece it falls perfectly into place as a sign for the lifetime I did a SR for this morning.

A cherry or cherries, in whichever way they appear to

me, are signs making me aware of Yvonne's involvement or connection to any specific situation, so this is a very apt piece of the jigsaw.

Now last night I was watching a film where they started to sing 'The Bonnie Banks o' Loch Lomond'. I was in floods of tears, so instantly felt that this was a sign. Ardlui and the Ardlui Hotel are situated on the banks of Loch Lomond. *The jigsaw is being pieced together perfectly*, I thought.

While staying at the Ardlui Hotel I walked down to the water's edge. During my walk I had connected to a part of my soul trapped in this past life with Yvonne's soul. The smell of cherry was a sign that this issue was connected to Yvonne's soul and that Ardlui, the hotel named after Mum, was a strong enough sign to get me to stay. Had the hotel been called anything else I do feel that I would have driven on by.

The feelings that surfaced after having read Yvonne's message were the feelings my soul's physical body felt in this lifetime that he experienced around this part of Loch Lomond.

As I drove to the sea this morning I was shown that our souls' physical bodies in this lifetime were meant to meet by the banks of the loch, but never did.

I will use the names Moira (Yvonne) and Jack (me) to make understanding this a little easier. Moira was going somewhere before going to meet Jack. Jack declined Moira's invitation to go with her and went to the loch, where he waited and waited, but Moira never arrived. Somewhere on the way to the loch something tragic happened and Moira was killed. When Jack found out he beat himself up and was unable to forgive himself for not going with Moira. If he had, perhaps he could have saved or rescued her.

However, as I now know, everything happens for a reason, specifically for our souls' experiences, but these were the feelings that the dog barking brought up in me. I now understand why I had to be so relaxed when the dog started barking to basically shock it out of me, which it did.

The SR took place by the sea, a body of water just like the loch. This was poetic, I feel. The sun was shining, I had the beach to myself, and after having chatted with that part of my soul who connected with me at Ardlui I was able to let him go easily.

I said to him, 'The sooner you let go and allow Archangel Azrael to escort you to a place of healing the sooner you will reconnect with the soul that resides within me. Your relationship with Moira and your thoughts that it could never be bettered, regarding the love you experienced, were misplaced. Once you reconnect with Shanti and me you will be absolutely blown out of the water, for the relationship that is about to enter our reality will be of the highest quality of love ever experienced. So hurry up and come back smartish.'

This worked, for I do feel that he had let go even before I got onto the beach. Good lad.

This whole experience has shone the light on why, since meeting Yvonne in this present lifetime, I have found it extremely difficult to say 'No,' when she has invited me to any sort of function or meditation. It was for fear of not being there if something were to ever happen to

Yvonne. In truth I can't remember ever saying 'No.' I do feel that this is part of the cycle to be ended.

As I have stated, I now know that where I am meant to be I will be for my soul's journey, and that if anything were to happen to Yvonne it was meant to be that way. It's my soul's journey as it is Yvonne's, and as it is your soul's journey to experience what is for our souls' best interest. This is regardless of who is with us at any point in our journey, or where we need to be. And this applies even to the times when we are on our own physically.

But in truth we are never alone. We have many friends in spirit with us always.

In the last two SR pieces we have tied up all the loose ends and have now allowed a beautiful soul to enter our life. After having experienced all those lifetimes of perceived tragedy and untimely endings, now is the time. It's my and Shanti's time to enjoy an unconditionally loving relationship. All the grief and heartache will fade away into nothingness when this lady enters our life. It will be so worth it.

And as each SR has been completed, both my mum's soul and Yvonne's will be feeling lighter and positive through my and Shanti's and my amazing SR teammates' efforts. For my part, I feel so honoured to be of service in this magical way.

It is a win–win–win situation for each one of us.

PS... Regarding the Lilford situation, do I go or not? This conundrum was answered today, 17th December

2021, during a quick but very important chat with Yvonne. On 21st December it is for me to go there as part of my soul's journey to bring yet another cycle to an end. And I'm going to do everything in my power to make sure that every cycle is ended before I and my soul shuffle off this mortal coil this time around.

It was finally completed on the spring equinox in March 2022 when I replied to a message from Yvonne almost immediately, declining her invitation to Lilford.

I was again drawn to the seaside and then in the afternoon to Rivington where Donna, a friend, and I were guided to do a SR and an EC clearing with such a powerful outcome for the area.

So again I was, as I always am, in the best place for my soul to evolve at all times.

The Pure Gold SR ~ from Around 2000 BCE to 22nd February 2022

As with Book One, I thought the last SR was to be the last piece. But hey, what do I know.

I have mentioned various cycles being ended that have been included within the SRs of the recent past. This SR is on the same wavelength but at a more profound and deeper level.

It has been my nemesis.

I have had ongoing issues with finance for as long as I can remember and done SR work on lifetimes involving money regarding lack and loss, but this one is a cycle specifically involving the precious metal gold.

For the last few days I have been gifted snippets of this cycle through a SR I did on Friday, and through visual signs on the TV. Virtually everything I saw on TV over the weekend involved gold, which is so pertinent to the issue at hand.

The SR on Friday involved a lifetime where my soul

was obsessed with money in general but gold especially, to the point where his marriage and his life took a back seat as his obsession took over his life completely. The obsessive behaviour expanded into paranoia during his continual accumulating of gold, which then multiplied the fear of someone stealing it from him.

This is just one lifetime of many regarding this cycle, I believe. I have been made aware of lifetimes in Egypt as a member of royalty, lifetimes as a pirate and a lifetime as this gentleman, which is the most recent incarnation I have been made aware of. I feel that there have been many lifetimes where I excavated for gold in various physical human forms and in various countries during this cycle. All this created a truly massive challenge for me to surrender to and to let go of these issues.

Lack: in the lifetimes I have been shown, as a member of royalty in Egypt, as a pirate and in general someone who is totally obsessed with gold and many other lifetimes yet unseen ... when I have accumulated a certain amount it seemed as if my soul's physical form never had enough so he continued to hoard, mine, buy or even steal it.

Loss: having hoarded gold in these lifetimes, fear has always been a silent harbinger of doom. The fear of someone taking or stealing my soul's booty was always lurking in the back of his mind. Hence the paranoia.

Forgiveness: forgiving every soul, including mine for the actions taken, which have led to me seeing this very toxic cycle or old pattern today, 10th January 2022. It hasn't been pretty, but we must accept our shadow side as well as our good side.

In each of these lifetimes my soul's single-mindedness caused problems for the many souls who played the roles of very close friends or loved ones. My soul treated them abysmally in those incarnations. I ask for and know that forgiveness has been gifted on both sides. Thank you all so much for your kindness.

This leads me to this morning, 10th January 2022. I was guided to go to the seaside but didn't want to. At these times I know that this is the very thing I need to do, though, and by doing so I will benefit greatly.

While driving I began to receive information regarding what I needed to do to bring this cycle to its timely completion. I must admit that it wasn't something I had thought of, but as I stilled my mind the information came clear. It was the perfect solution or action to clear this cycle.

I was to return a small one-gramme gold bar to the sea. This cost £50. After my initial reticence I had a few moments of contemplation before asking my angelic friends to infuse the bar with their divine energies, so that when I returned the gold bar back into the ocean it would be infused with positive energies to help with the process of Gaia or Mother Earth's healing.

While it would help me release and surrender this most challenging issue, it would also benefit all souls upon this planet and beyond. I had to take these actions to physically show that I was ready to let go of this obsession and to realise that as I let go I would open myself to the flow of the universe regarding finance, be it through receipt of money or gold. It would be a massive win–win for me personally.

And, for the collective I am part of, it will mean that

my actions will filter out around the world and beyond to every soul. When a ripple is sent out it travels far and wide. Whether it is a positive or negative action, a word spoken or a thought, it will ripple out into the universe and connect with every soul.

Now my mind and my ego had worked out how much I was going to lose by taking this action. If I went by the original price I paid I would lose £50, which is not to be sniffed at. But if the gold bar ever became more valuable, then I would be throwing away more money, which would be quite a sum for anyone.

Once I had removed these material thoughts I focused on the benefits, which were:

The ending of this cycle for me personally.

The opening of the floodgates for me to receive true abundance in all forms.

The fact that I will feel much more at peace after having taken this action.

I will have helped my universal brothers and sisters.

These all completely outweighed the selfishness I would have felt, had I kept the gold bar.

I returned the gold bar to the ocean with thanks and gratitude for being able to play a part in this experience and was further blessed as I started to walk along the beach. I was gifted a vision of a mermaid waving at me, who had come to collect the gold bar. When seeing this I did feel quite emotional, knowing this was confirmation that this cycle had come to a very fitting end.

I did have further challenges regarding this topic but succeeded in dealing with each challenge as it arose, until the day came when a cheque arrived on 22nd February, signalling to me that I had achieved completion.

I thank God/Goddess, my soul retrieval teammates, guides, angels, and ancestors for your support today, in the past and more so in each now moment. Thank you. This SR piece really is an apt way of completing my SR journey for now.

Each SR experience has been pure gold.

The Remember 'The Promise You Made' SR ~ September 1999 to 10th February 2022

THIS REVOLVES AROUND a soul experience or cycle that Dad's soul and mine agreed to play out over many lifetimes. I have through signs been reminded of this via a song written by/for a pop group called Cock Robin. The song is entitled 'The Promise You Made'. My soul had obviously agreed to keep this promise this time around, and with the information I have received since Friday my soul Shanti and I are now in a prime position to do the necessary work to bring this cycle to an end.

This is an end to a particularly unpleasant experience, perhaps the worst earth experience we can ever have, but one in which Dad's soul and mine have played both parts – both causer and victim.

Therefore, I can forgive completely, having achieved a level of spirituality and knowing the truth of everything we experience here on earth. All this is coming to fruition on a most auspicious day, 10th February 2022, when six years ago to the day, I experienced the worst day of my life.

Dad was well into the final part of his life, having had a stroke in 2008 that which expanded into dementia and what I now know to be a deep hatred of himself for what he caused me and my brother Jack to experience.

Dad set in motion a series of events through his actions that hours later led to me losing my home, my job and Dad all in one go.

Before I continue with all the information I received about this family issue, I want to say that not only did I find it easy to forgive, but in the here and now I feel the pain Dad has carried with him and simply wish to help him ease it.

The love I have for my dad has gone to a higher level, if indeed there could be a higher level. I love my dad and have the deepest respect for him and his soul journey. Being able to play a part to help him is an honour, for it will set both our souls truly free to enjoy the rest of our soul journey without the excess baggage that no longer serves either of us.

Dad's soul has been and still is one of my greatest spiritual teachers, which I am truly grateful for. Indeed his soul is by my side as I type, helping me from the realm of spirit.

I wish to expand on the auspiciousness of today's date. As I have said, six years ago to the day this issue began, and now six years later it will be ended. And the numbers add up to six in the year 2022. It's all about karma, and today we balance that karma. Is this divinely timed or what?

When receiving information this morning, I didn't

fully understand what was being asked of me. I simply felt an overwhelming wave of emotion surge up and out of me via many tears. As the day evolved I understood where these emotions were coming from. They were a combination of Dad's and mine. Dad had suppressed his emotions for a very long time, nearly sixty years. I can only try to imagine the emotions he felt when realising what he had caused Jack and me to experience.

This explains why he was never able to express his emotions: he didn't feel worthy of help or love. So he tried to go it alone and did a heck of a job, but this took its toll on him and created lots of disharmony within his body that led to his many ailments later in life.

There is another song that epitomises Dad's and my relationship to a tee. It's a U2 song called 'Sometimes You Can't Make It on Your Own'. Since first hearing this song I have shed many a tear, but it has been necessary to bring up these emotions for me to release at intervals. My and your physical body can only cope with so much physical, mental and emotional releasing at one time. As I played it this morning I realised that Dad's message to me was a powerful one. He was telling me not to go through life as he had, trying to do it alone.

This too was perfectly timed because I have tried to go it alone, not wanting to ask for help as I felt that doing so meant I had failed in some way. This is untrue as I know now, also feeling unworthy, but now thankfully I realise that these feelings were as much Dad's as mine. To have this information has lifted a great weight from my shoulders. I just pray that any releasing I do here on in is pain-free.

I have felt at times since Dad passed that our lives have been full of regret. This feeling was more Dad's than mine, as I have worked on the regret I held on to. To help Dad become free of the constraints he had chained himself in is part of the promise my soul made. This SR is in motion as I type.

Archangel Michael is assisting this SR as he severs the cords of attachment to these painful emotions that had attached themselves to me. To help release these emotions on Dad's behalf is another part of the promise. Archangel Raphael is making sure these cords never reattach. Thank you both so much for your help.

Whatever Dad and I have been through in this present life and whatever our souls have experienced for a lot longer, I have viewed this lifetime as having been a life full of regret, anger, sadness and despair. I am truly blessed to have experienced this part of my journey with you, Dad. I love you so much. Thank you for your help and your love.

The real Brucie Bonus is the realisation that from the moment I was born Dad and I were at loggerheads constantly. Yet for all our many unpleasant experiences, intermingled with some good times (albeit too short-lived), the one thing that was always constant but alas invisible was and is the love we had for each other without even being aware of it.

This is a true gift, which now releases the illusion that I have always felt about our life together being a waste of time. It has been a blessed and very sacred lifetime with untold blessings, which Dad, our ancestors and I will benefit from greatly now.

The SR was concluded as I wrote this piece. Thanking every angel present, for your help in bringing this cycle to the perfect end at the perfect time.

Additional information came to me today, 13th February 2022.

As I was driving to the seaside I started to get information through regarding this cycle and what still needed attending to. Mum made herself known via a vision of her face, both yesterday and today, so I knew Mum was there to help but that she was also there to make me aware of the issues and the emotions I was releasing on her behalf.

Mum's situation was completely different to mine and Dad's. Mum was between a rock and a hard place when this scenario began to play out all those years ago. Mum, while knowing what was happening to Jack and me, had a very difficult decision to make. Should she tell someone about what has been going on? This would undoubtedly have had consequences for Dad. Or should she keep quiet, and hope that it would go away?

It's easy for someone to say what mum should have done. But, with the greatest of respect, until you or I have been in this position we are in no position to judge Mum's choice or indeed judge anyone who is faced with this or any sort of tough decision.

Mum, God bless her, chose to keep quiet. However, this caused Mum great turmoil within and she felt indecisive for many years, perhaps until her last breath.

I now believe that this situation was a major cause of her many illnesses, especially the cancer.

I also had the feeling that the trapped soul involved within this issue had very recently been able to show himself to me and was now seeking help to be set free from this unpleasant illusion.

The soul involved was the soul who resided in my physical body at the time of my birth and stayed until 1999 when, as I have mentioned before, another soul, Shanti, walked-in as the previous soul left to seek another body to continue his soul journey.

The SR I was to set in motion was that of the soul who experienced this unpleasant situation while residing within my body and taking on the physical and emotional baggage that came with it.

This soul and my physical body experienced this situation in two ways.

1. The first was to help my physical body prepare for the arrival of another soul, Shanti, and to help Shanti release all the spiritual baggage that he had collated over many lifetimes. If Shanti was able to release his spiritual baggage, which was connected to the same sort of experiences that I had had as a child, and if my physical body were able to release its own baggage at the same precise moment, we would then be able to clear it all completely.
2. For me the second was also an opportunity to end this cycle for myself and my ancestors. Success has been achieved on both counts.

Now the way any cycle is ended is simple. One soul involved in any cycle must act by not taking action. What I mean is this: while this cycle of unpleasantness continued for me and my family, the souls involved hadn't reached the awareness to realise that what we do unto others we do unto ourselves.

I have been blessed with such a true miracle for this physical body. Despite all that it has experienced emotionally, mentally and physically via abuse it is still in a healthy state. This is a sign that this cycle was being readied to be ended in this present lifetime.

As I became more spiritually aware and as I remember who I am, going deeper into my personal healing journey, I became more aware that everything I say, do and think has a direct bearing on those close to me. This then sends ripples out into the universe, be they negative or positive.

This is the same for you. Any thought, word-spoken or action will ripple out into the universe, affecting every soul, depending on the vibration sent out.

As I have said often, we are all connected, we are all one.

So on Friday 4th February 2022 I reflected on everything I had remembered and all the self-work I have done over the last twenty years, especially regarding compassion and forgiveness. And then came the understanding that no amount of revenge or retaliation could ever satisfy my lust for justice.

I realised that it could never balance what I had searched for, when in the past I had sought revenge for what had happened to me or Shanti. When my awareness and level of healing came to this point I was then ready to receive the information about Dad and the abuse that took place without getting angry and without being vengeful. Instead my initial reaction was to physically say to Dad, 'I forgive you,' as I forgave Mum and the other souls involved, including myself.

Now it will take a little time to completely forgive, but I put in motion these words to bring closure for every soul involved, especially mine. The more I say these words the quicker absolute forgiveness will be attained.

This is what Jesus has said to me many times:

'Forgiveness must be absolute. To forgive, we must forgive every soul everything it has caused us or that our soul has caused them, however abhorrent the experience has been. These actions and words alone will break these cycles.'

So, with my knowledge of spirituality, I had been given an opportunity to use all that Shanti and I have remembered, to use in a way that creates no further karma and sets all souls involved free from this cycle.

However, those involved with the cycle will have their own healing journey to oversee, whatever they have caused other souls to experience. But by seeking no retaliation or revenge I, with Shanti's help, have chosen to let go, to forgive and to move on. After all, I have set myself free, and personally that's the main thing I focus on. The fact that other souls are set free too is a bonus.

Had I stayed on this spiritual merry-go-round, seeking revenge on Dad, I know a hundred per cent that I would have caused more souls and physical bodies to experience more unpleasant actions and would have also created more karma for myself.

The question I ask is this:
Is it worth it? My reply is a categorical 'No.'

However, until you (or someone who is involved in a cycle of unpleasantness that you are experiencing) attain a spiritual awareness about what I have written above, you will undoubtedly keep going around in circles, experience lifetime after lifetime of this experience and create more pain and suffering.

This reason, and this alone, is why I have added this piece and this SR.

By working on ourselves and opening to the truth of who we are spiritually, by forgiving, by surrendering any negative thoughts, by refraining from carrying out actions that will cause others to suffer and by no longer seeking retaliation or revenge... These are the only ways we can change the world.

I am truly grateful to my beloved Dad, Mum, Jack and all other souls involved within our now extinct experience for the pain and suffering I and my ancestors have experienced, which will hopefully give you the impetus to view and change your future to a future without suffering.

Now isn't that a world worth manifesting?

The releasing I have done on behalf of Mum and Dad during the unveiling of this experience are the emotions and feelings that Mum (for forty years) and Dad (for fifty years) have inadvertently imprinted on me during this lifetime. This is something my soul agreed to. While it has been painful and unpleasant, I am honoured to be able to do this for my immediate family and ancestors. May you all be free to experience more pleasant experiences now, dear family.

I have also been made aware regarding my physical body that in the past I have berated myself for the shape it has been in. But today, with all that my physical body has coped with throughout this lifetime, I see the truth of this lifetime and its many challenges. As I have written earlier, I now choose to stop beating myself up and just offer so much gratitude that my body is as healthy as it is.

I now love myself.

The Ancestral & Reptilian SR ~ Date Unknown to 10th March 2022

I HAVE JUST completed a most amazing SR involving my ancestors and the reptilians who were once embedded within my ancestors' physical bodies during this prolonged karmic cycle, which has spanned thousands of years.

During another healing at Yvonne's yesterday, information came through about an unpleasant happening connected to my most recent ancestors – namely, my dad and my granddad. This situation, while unpleasant, allowed me the opportunity to accrue new and deeper understanding, and I am now able to forgive all my ancestors for the roles they played within this cycle.

On my way home last night I felt slightly out of kilter when seeing a car with the letters SAM on the registration plate. Sam was my granddad. I knew the way I was feeling had something to do with him.

Early the next morning I felt a wave of energy flow into me. I didn't feel anything untoward so went back to sleep. However, having just ended the SR for these souls this afternoon, I have been made aware that it was Archangel Michael who stepped into my being this morning in preparation for this SR work. This tells me that the SR my SR teammates and I were to do was a very powerful one, and so it has proved.

I had many thoughts regarding what I was going to do today, be it going to the cinema, visiting a crystal shop or going to the seaside, but I did none of them. I now know that I had to prepare my home for an amazing SR with many souls, both ancestral and reptilian beings. My experiences with our reptilian brothers and sisters have shown them to be energetic beings rather than having a physical body like we humans. This is how they show themselves to me. To others they may look or feel energetically different.

I prepared quite meticulously, as I do when SR work calls – lighting candles, playing angelic music, cleansing with sage and removing any electrical items from the room. I really made sure that the connection I was seeking would be as pure and truthful as it could be.

I had no idea how many trapped souls were there as I began, and I only spoke to my granddad. Then more of my ancestors came in as I spoke. At one point the reptilians started to come in too. I felt that my ancestors were standing on my left and the reptilians on my right.

While speaking about forgiving themselves for what they had done or had done to them, I urged them not to seek revenge when they saw the truth of their experiences. I suddenly said, 'Will my ancestors and the reptilians turn to face each other?'

I asked them to look each other in the eyes and hold

the intention to send love to those they were facing. As I did this the line of both my ancestors and reptilians stretched as far as my spiritual vision allowed me to see. There were many more ancestors and reptilians involved within this cycle than I could ever imagine. Hence this was why Archangel Michael stepped into my physical body to work through me during this remarkable experience. I was really flabbergasted at the enormity of this cycle and number of souls involved, but also so honoured to play my part to help bring down the curtain on this cycle.

Each ancestor involved with this unpleasant cycle had been impregnated by a reptilian, the same reptilian's facing my ancestors right here right now.

This was a SR of forgiveness on a major scale. No one was able to move on without this forgiveness. As I have already written, the reptilians have been controlled in a much worse way than we humans have. Yet as they awaken now, one by one raising their consciousness through my SR team's help and others, they will begin to see who they truly are. When people say we are ascending this isn't only for humans. It is for every soul throughout God/Goddess's created realm and it includes reptilians and other species too. We cannot ascend if even one soul is left behind.

My message to every soul on that part of their journey when they too begin to awaken is that I urge them to forgive their souls for any unpleasantness they have experienced. I beat myself up greatly for many years when I saw what my soul had experienced through a myriad of different physical forms.

I repeat: our soul is on a journey, and it uses this

physical form, be it a fish, a bird, a tree, a man or a woman to have the experiences it has chosen while here on earth.

What a truly amazing SR to complete Book Two with. Thank you, angels.

The next piece will give more detail about forgiveness.

A Message from Jesus

JESUS HAS BEEN inviting me to channel this piece on his behalf for a while now. However, as with all things, everything happens at the perfect time.

> Forgiveness must be absolute.

This means that, as we learn to forgive, we will do well to remember this statement, for Jesus lovingly advises us to forgive everyone and everything completely. Hence the word *absolute*. So whatever anyone does or has done, said or thought in the past or present or may do in the future, however abhorrent an experience you can think of, we are all best served by starting a process of forgiveness rather than being judgemental, getting angry or even seeking to cause harm to anyone in any way.

Because whatever is occurring in any person's life, they really are doing their best. So rather than judging them, if their actions directly or indirectly affect us or our loved ones, please heed these words, for Jesus again invites us to repel any thoughts of retaliation or seeking revenge.

If their actions have caused unpleasantness, this can be traced back more often than not to something that has caused pain or suffering to them or their loved ones. If we go back to the very first action or the very first word said or thought within this situation, we will see that it automatically set in motion a karmic cycle that will only cease when those involved are able to begin the process of forgiveness. This will lead to us forgiving each other completely.

We can only work on ourselves. So if we are able to forgive, we set ourselves free from any specific cycle. Those still involved and unable to forgive will continue to experience this issue in various ways until they too can learn to forgive. It's all part of the soul's journey.

If for any reason you or I were to retaliate or seek revenge we would incur karma, which we would have to work through ourselves. So, to save ourselves a lot of heartache, the only way to go is to forgive, to let go of any judgement whatsoever and to accept everyone for who they are, knowing they are doing their best. I know this can be the hardest thing to do, especially if, as I have said, any action or word spoken hurts a cherished family member or dear friend.

Jesus urges us to call upon him in these times for the strength and compassion to forgive, encompassed in love, to help release the pain we are holding on to.

Everything I write about I have experienced to a very extreme degree, so I can therefore share my experiences to help you break the barrier of illusion, for what we do unto others we do unto ourselves. We are all connected. We are all one.

I will add an example of that, which over the last few weeks has come to the fore. It was a very unpleasant experience – perhaps, some may say, the worst. I have recently come to understand, through healing and inner work, that an experience happened to my brother Jack and me as infants, leading to a very unpleasant end for my brother. Thankfully I survived.

When at Yvonne's, while we were talking in general, this topic popped into my mind to ask about. And later during the chat it transpired that some unpleasant experiences had befallen my brother Jack and me.

Information had filtered through to me about this over the last few years, but I was unable to believe or didn't want to believe that these things had happened. But in Yvonne's healing room I had nowhere to hide. Confirmation came through very clearly, so I accepted what had happened and forgave everyone involved completely, including myself.

My first words were, 'I forgive Dad for whatever he did,' and I also wished that he would forgive himself. No anger surfaced. I simply wished that this issue be healed with forgiveness being offered absolutely. And this I did, for there is no benefit from holding a grudge. We will all have a better life in front of us if only we let go of what is behind us.

A very simple affirmation to say (as and when you feel drawn to it) is, 'I forgive.' Say this often, and as many times as you need to.

Perhaps you may be wondering how can you forgive so easily.

I have worked hard since awakening to my spirituality of who I truly am in 2003. I am a being of love and light having a temporary earth experience, exactly as you are.

I have learnt through many opportunities that this is the best way forward.

We cannot change the past and what has occurred. As Archangel Michael often says, 'There is no point crying over spilt milk,' and finally I understand what he means.

If I were to get angry, violent or seek revenge, which I have done in past lifetimes, I would only be hurting myself and would cause more karma for myself in the process in this lifetime.

Now I know that I would be sabotaging my present and my future for something that happened in the past that cannot be changed, why would I do that? It was a eureka moment when this realisation hit home, but it is the truth. Even before I awakened to a spiritual path in this present lifetime I had subconsciously been guided to refrain from any retaliation whatsoever, involving various situations. I am so glad.

And while some may think that people get away with their actions, they don't.

Karma has been created in a way that we need not get involved. Just by knowing karma is a part of our soul's journey to help those who cause suffering and pain however extreme by giving them further experiences in which to learn to react differently, however long it takes to realise, for karma itself is no bad thing.

It offers us another opportunity to change how we would react if or when another similar situation

Lightning Source UK Ltd.
Milton Keynes UK
UKHW052138140822
407233UK00009B/451